CRITIC

CW00746714

ADULTS, KIDS AND TEENS

The Complete Guide to Increase Your Critical Thinking Skills, Powerful Techniques for Problem Solving, and Improve Your Social Skills

Emily Campbell

Table of Contents

Legal & Disclaimer

The information contained in this book and its contents is not designed to replace or take the place of any form of medical or professional advice; and is not meant to replace the need for independent medical, financial, legal or other professional advice or services, as may be required. The content and information in this book has been provided for educational and entertainment purposes only.

The content and information contained in this book has been compiled from sources deemed reliable, and it is accurate to the best of the Author's knowledge, information and belief. However, the Author cannot guarantee its accuracy and validity and cannot be held liable for any errors and/or omissions. Further, changes are periodically made to this book as and when needed. Where appropriate and/or necessary, you must consult a professional (including but not limited to your doctor, attorney, financial advisor or such other professional advisor) before using any of the suggested remedies, techniques, or information in this book.

Upon using the contents and information contained in this book, you agree to hold harmless the Author from and against any damages, costs, and expenses, including any legal fees potentially resulting from the application of any of the information provided by this book. This disclaimer applies to any loss, damages or injury caused by the use and application, whether directly or indirectly, of any advice or information presented, whether for breach of contract, tort, negligence, personal injury, criminal intent, or under any other cause of action.

You agree to accept all risks of using the information presented inside this book.

You agree that by continuing to read this book, where appropriate and/or necessary, you shall consult a professional (including but not limited to your doctor, attorney, or financial advisor or such other advisor as needed) before using any of the suggested remedies, techniques, or information in this book.

Introduction

Critical thinking is a process that is very involved in gaining understanding, gaining knowledge, and solving problems. The method of critical thinking requires an open mind when gathering and analyzing data to consider many possible solutions to the questions raised. The process requires a thorough evaluation of each likely answer for the probability of accuracy. The critical thinking process is accomplished by picking the answer with the highest probability of precision.

For example, thinking is something we all do. There are likely variations in our thought from our prejudices and distorted views. The prejudices or skewed perceptions may be based on assumptions that we have made and facts that we have accepted as true. Questioning our assumptions and the information given to us will help us carry out assessments that may foster our ability to gain value from our thinking. Because our thought outcomes determine how effective we are to be, it is very necessary to improve our ability to think

This development we want is a process that requires much work. No matter the will, it is impossible to become a critical thinker overnight. It is a challenging long-term process. It might even take a couple of years just to change our thinking habits. The vital and ideal characteristics of a real critical thinker require an even longer period to reach full development.

As you read this book, you will be given a brief introduction to critical thinking—you will discover the core critical thinking skills. You will see what someone who is capable of critical thinking may look like, contrasted with the behaviors of someone who is not so critical at thinking. You will learn about the benefits, as well as several obstacles that may make critical thinking difficult. You will be given some steps to prime your body to be a critical thinker, and you will be guided through the critical thinking process. You will also learn about the importance of raising a critically thinking child, as well as how to ensure that your child develops those important skills. Finally, you will be provided with several exercises that will enable you to boost your own current critical thinking skills.

There are plenty of books on this subject on the market, thanks again for choosing this one! Every effort was made to ensure it is full of as much useful information as possible. Please enjoy!

Chapter One: What is Critical Thinking?

Imagine that you are at home with your four young children aged 7, 5, 3, and 5 months old. They are all currently crying, and you need to figure out what order to help them in—the infant is crying because she has a dirty diaper, and it is time for her to drink her milk. The 7-year-old is crying because he jumped off of a desk, hit his head, and is bleeding. The 3-year-old is crying because the episode of his favorite television show has ended, and you need to go select a new one for him, and the 5-year-old is crying because she says everyone is too loud and her head hurts. What order do you handle the children?

7 year old boy

•Crying becuase he is hurt and bleeding after hitting head

5 year old girl

•Crying because she has a headache from all the crying of her siblings

3 year old boy

•Crying because he wants more television

5 month old girl

•Crying because she has a dirty diaper and is hungry

It can be hard to figure out the best way to juggle the chaos in your home at that moment—you have a child bleeding profusely, a child with a headache, a child who wants help with something relatively unimportant, and an infant in a dirty diaper who needs you to nurse her, requiring you to stop and sit down for at least 20 minutes. You could do things by age—working from the youngest up to finally helping the oldest with his head injury after meeting the needs of everyone else, or you could go with helping your oldest first and helping the younger ones later. Ultimately, you need to figure out the best order to handle everything in a reasonable manner that leaves everyone as well-taken-care-of as possible.

This is where critical thinking comes in. When you are able to think critically, you are able to gather information quickly—you are able to look around that room filled with sobbing children and figure out exactly why everyone is crying in an instant. In gathering that information, you can start to rank it in order of most to least important—in this case, it is most likely going to involve you first checking on the child who is bleeding to make sure it is not severe enough for a hospital visit and getting him all patched up, so he is not getting blood on everything. At that point, you would most likely change the diaper of the baby, then fix the television before settling down to feed the baby. Doing this then directly solves the 5-year-old's problem because she was bothered by all the crying, and once you have tended to everyone else and solved all of their reasons for crying, you calm her down as well. Suddenly, you are sitting in a room with four happy children again, all thanks to your ability to go through the information rationally.

Notice how, during this, you went through several steps, even in the instant that it happened. You first assessed the situation—you have now gathered all the necessary

12

information. Then, you were able to conceptualize it—
everyone is crying for a reason, and they are all
distinctly separate problems. You are then able to
analyze by importance—you need to make sure that the
oldest child is not severely injured first and foremost
because head wounds can warrant emergency room
visits if they are severe enough. Then, you need to
ensure that your infant does not sit in a dirty diaper that
could lead to a rash. At that point, you still have an
infant that needs to be fed, but doing so will leave the
other two children endlessly crying until you finished, so
you take the thirty seconds to fix the television. It made
the most sense to fix the show then because doing so
will ensure that the middle two children stop crying, and
really your infant waiting an extra minute for food is not
the end of the world. In the end, the problems were
handled in the most effective way possible to ensure that
everyone's needs were met.

Essentially, when you are thinking critically, you are
assessing, analyzing, and acting. Each of these requires
you to think effectively and ensure that you are rational,
critical, and open-minded, making the decision that is
appropriate for the situation that you have found yourself

in. You will be able to do several things—you will show an inclination to behave in ways that are inherently problem-solving oriented. You will be intelligent. You will be able to make rational, logical decisions. Effectively, you will be able to understand and interact with the world around you in a way that is deemed to be intelligent and functional.

Types of Critical Thinking

You may find that you utilize critical thinking in several different situations—you may use critical thinking when trying to solve a problem, such as the one given to you earlier. You may use critical thinking skills to infer information that is not directly said but is heavily implied, such as someone giving several answers to why they are hesitant to do something and being able to infer that the answer is no. You may use it to disprove that click-bait article you scrolled past on social media that took a quote out of context and ran with it to make someone else look bad. You may use it to figure out why a code that you have written is not functioning or to figure out what has died in your car by process of elimination.

When you are trying to think critically, you are trying to gain further information about something so you can make an informed decision. This usually involves going through several thought processes to arrive at that point. This can happen in several different ways. In fact, there are several different forms of critical thinking that are all related, and in some cases, overlapping in nature. Some forms of critical thinking include:

- Anthropological or sociological thinking

- Historical thinking

- Legal thinking

- Logical thinking

- Mathematical thinking

- Musical thinking

- Political thinking

- Psychological thinking

- Philosophical or ethical thinking

- Scientific thinking

In looking over those forms, what stands out? Can you identify a way that these may all be similar to each other? What do they have in common? If you can answer what they all have in common, you are already using critical thinking skills—you are using your background knowledge surrounding these subjects to find patterns, make inferences, and apply that information.

In this case, what all of these have in common is that they look like they all belong in a college course listing—for a good reason. These are all considered academic fields. Academics tend to very heavily be swayed by critical thinking, even when they may not seem like it. Art history, for example, has just as much critical thinking value as taking a class on philosophy or biology—you are still going to be gathering information, interpreting that information, and then applying that information to make informed, educated conclusions on the information that has been given to you. Critical thinking skills determine your ability to be successful in an academic setting because academics themselves are so focused on learning, exploring, and interpreting.

Most of the time, the first form of critical thinking that children become aware of, or at least the first one they may think of when cued to think about it, is the scientific method, and it does a fantastic job at summing up what critical thinking is all about. When you are taught the scientific method, you are given six steps to follow in order to explore the world around you that happen in a never-ending cycle—you observe, hypothesize, test and gather results, analyze the results, and then either accept or reject the hypothesis that you have posited. In general, you are going to continue this cycle until you find an equilibrium between your hypothesis and your end results.

Why Critical Thinking Matters

These skills may seem abstract—after all, do you really need to be able to recite the scientific method or know what modus ponens is and how to use it in order to be effective in real-life scenarios? Some people may incorrectly assume that, just like teachers used to say that you need to learn how to do math by hand because you will not always have a calculator on hand, being able to use these critical thinking skills is something that is said to be needed but not actually relevant. After all, when is the last time that you have used the equation to identify the area of a circle or needed the quadratic formula after you have graduated from high school or college?

Most people never use these skills again—if they are not directly relevant to their job, they will not need them. An artist may not need to know the area of a circle or how to make a perfect argument that is foolproof, so those critical thinking skills seem irrelevant. If an artist does not need to be thinking about abstract or concrete data, do they really need to be able to think critically?

The answer is yes—critical thinking is critical for a reason. These skills can be relevant in nearly any setting. You may not need to use math skills, but the skills behind those math skills, the fundamental critical thinking skills, are crucial and will be used again and again. You will use these skills in your relationships—

such as when you need to make a compromise over something that you may feel quite passionately about but cannot get your partner to agree on. You may use them when trying to decide which car to get when your old one dies, or when trying to figure out which job makes the most sense for you. You will be able to create patterns and inferences based on smaller sums of information in ways that will be relevant to you in basic life.

Consider grocery shopping for a moment. You may go into the store with a concrete list in hand with a plan to get exactly what you came for and nothing else. As you look at your first item, you see that what you need to get is tomato sauce, so you go to the canned aisle and look at the sauce. Suddenly, you realize that not only are there several different brands of sauce, but also different sizes of cans for the same brands of sauce. How do you know which one makes the most sense for you to buy? The smaller cans may look cheaper at a glance, but are they really? The larger cans cost more for the can, but if you look closely at the prices compared to what you get, you may realize something—it pays to buy in bulk. The larger cans of tomato sauce are usually slightly cheaper per ounce.

To see this, think about it this way: Your recipe calls for 24 oz. of tomato sauce. You can buy cans of 8 oz. of tomato sauce for $0.49 each, or you can buy cans of 16 oz. of tomato sauce for $0.85, or you can buy cans of 30 oz. of tomato sauce for $1.39 each. Now, let's add up the cost per oz. of each of these—this is quite simple. All you will need to do is divide the price of the can by the oz. within the can to get the price per oz.

When you do this, you find out that buying an 8 oz. can results in you effectively paying $0.0612/oz. while buying a 16 oz. can costs you $0.05312/oz., and buying a 30 oz. can of sauce will cost you $0.046333/oz.

With some critical thinking skills, you can now figure out that it makes the most sense per oz. to buy the largest can of sauce, even if you are not going to use the whole thing. In order to buy the exact amount of sauce, you would have to buy three cans of the 8 oz. sauce, and you would spend $1.47. Even with you throwing away a small amount of sauce in buying a 30 oz. can, you are still only spending $1.39 for that can as opposed to $1.47 to get an exact amount with smaller numbers.

While a few cents may not seem like a big deal, this can add up exponentially. If you start to shop around and figure out the ways to buy food that are cheaper, your food budget can go down, thanks to your ability to use your critical thinking skills in a way that is meaningful and beneficial to you. Ultimately, everyone has to eat, and food will almost always be an added cost unless you happen to be a serious homesteader that is able to produce everything you ever use at home. This means that critical thinking skills are relevant to you in some way, even if you are not going to be working in a field that is largely technical, mathematical, or scientific.

Chapter Two: Core Critical Thinking Skills are a Proven Path to the Success of Students

From tackling classroom assignments to dealing with real-world problems, critical thinking is a powerful and valuable skill for students to possess. Instead of accepting their reasoning as all the proof they need, students should instead use critical thinking to analyze the way they think. They should also be able to provide sufficient evidence for their concepts. By mastering critical thinking skills, students can gain numerous benefits, such as empathy for different points of view and better control of their learning abilities.

It is essential for students' future that they learn and develop their ability to consider a problem or situation and think it through from all angles. To do this, they need to improve their ability to think critically. Nowadays, education systems are failing in certain parts of the world because they do not take this aspect of learning, also referred to as the art of thinking about thinking, as seriously as they should. Of course, the challenge is to create learning environments that encourage and facilitate critical thinking in the classroom and other places. Learning and practicing critical thinking allows students to take charge and embrace heir learning. Usually, students who do this tend to approach their coursework effectively and thoughtfully, participate more intensely in the learning process, and ask more relevant and challenging questions. Also, the art of critical thinking endures beyond the classroom and into adulthood and the workplace.

Due to the numerous proven benefits of critical thinking, it has become a standard course in university and college settings today. This process incorporates how students develop and apply their thought process to understand how thinking can go through expansion and improvement. Individuals are usually considered critical thinkers to the extent that they regularly improve their thinking ability intentionally. The basic concept behind the study of critical thinking is to determine weaknesses and strengths and make necessary improvements by dealing with the weak areas.

The word critical does not imply negativity; rather, it denotes the evaluation of judgments, ideas, or thought with creativity, awareness, and refinement of this process as required. Critical thinking is rooted in the work of prominent individuals such as Isaac Newton, Socrates, Rene Descartes, and Thomas Aquinas in its earlier times. Jean Piaget, Ludwig Wittgenstein, John Dewey, and others made more contributions that are modern. However, Robert Ennis's work gave rise to the skills taught in schools and reflected in the workplace.

Developing Critical Thinking in Children

Developing critical thinking skills in children does not need to be as intimidating as you may think! When you wish to encourage your children to grow up to be good, natural critical thinkers, you can do so with just a few tweaks to how you approach life, questions, and interactions with your children. Just a few changes can be enough over a childhood to push your child in the right direction to be the critical thinker that you know he or she can be.

Many parents dread the "why" phase when every statement is met with curiosity. The child may ask the parent why dogs walk funny, and you may answer that they are quadrupedal by nature. They may follow that up with the dreaded "Why?" and leave you scrambling for an answer. You may not necessarily know why so many animals evolved to be on four legs, or why humans happened to shift over to walking on two legs, and it can be incredibly easy to brush off your child's question and tell him that you do not know. However, these questions are the perfect opportunity to begin developing the critical thinking that your child will need as an adult. Instead of dismissing your child, encourage the questions. Encourage your child to think about why they think that dogs might walk on four legs instead of two, or ask why your child thinks that humans may use two hands. You may be surprised—even young children may be able to piece together that if they walked on four feet, they would not have hands to use for tools and games!

Encourage creativity, curiosity, and always follow up on the question and exploration stage with discovering the answer as well. This helps your child learn to think about theories, experiment, and then learn about how to research as well, all in one fell swoop that is encouraged by your critical thinking skills. When your child is wrong about an answer, you can also encourage your child to continue thinking about why they may be wrong or how they could change their assumptions to fit better and try again.

Learning from Others

Sometimes, what your child needs to do is use other sources to answer those questions that are brewing in her head. If your child is asking you why cars work the way they do and you happen to know a mechanic, for example, encourage your child to call up the mechanic, with your supervision, and ask questions, or go visit your mechanic friend so he can talk to her directly. Do not hesitate to pull in examples from books, videos, the internet, friends, family, or even experts at a museum or a zoo to answer those questions that are hard to figure out. Not only are you encouraging your child to learn how to use resources effectively, you are also teaching your child that it is okay to reach out to others when you do not have the knowledge that you would otherwise like to provide for him or her.

Help Evaluate Information

Sometimes, your child may feel overwhelmed with all of the information suddenly dumped on him during this process of learning how to think critically, and that is okay. What you can do during these times of feeling overwhelmed is to encourage your child to begin evaluating information. For example, if your child comes home upset one day and tells you that his friend has told him that Santa Claus is not real, you may use this as an opportunity to guide your child through evaluation. Ask your child what he thinks about that matter, encouraging him to figure out what he thinks. Ask why he thinks that way and why his friend happened to say what he did. Through the process, you can guide your child through beginning to evaluate the information and compare it to what your child already knows. In doing so, you can help your child begin to learn the foundation for evaluating the information being presented to him. In this process, you then help him learn how best to manage the information that is thrown his way at any given time.

Promote Learning Interests

Sometimes, though you may be bored to death over your child's most recent obsession, it is important to encourage those interests. Your child is naturally absorbing all sorts of information, and in encouraging her to follow her favorite interests, you are encouraging her to look at what she likes and why she likes it. You are also going to find that she is far more willing to become engaged in discussion, problem-solving, and experimenting when it is about a topic that she cares about. Though you may be bored to tears over trains, you should recognize that it is not about you and the fact that your child is so readily dedicating her time to learning and reading about trains means that she is becoming passionate about learning, and that is a fantastic life skill to develop. Following her lead with her favorite topics means that you will be able to ensure that you always have a willing participant when you are trying to teach critical thinking.

Use Problem-Solving Regularly

Guide your child through problem-solving while also talking it out when you do. You want to make sure that your child is able to learn this foundation as well as possible, as problem-solving is one of those skills that is always relevant. You can guide your child through problem-solving when appropriate, such as if your child is upset that there is only one cookie left, but there are two children, you could ask your child what she thinks would be the best way to fix the problem. Many children would stop, look, and recognize that sharing seems to be the most appropriate decision to make in that instance. It solves the problem by making sure that everyone gets a piece of cookie, and no one is left out. When she does not come up to that conclusion herself, you can guide her there through your own questions as well.

Good Listening Skills and Critical Thinking

Beyond just encouraging your child to develop critical thinking, it is important that other skills can directly impact an ability to think critically in the first place. Particularly important is the ability to listen well. A child who knows how to listen and understand as opposed to simply mindlessly obey without ever thinking about what is being requested is a child who has a good foundation for critical thinking, and if you can encourage your child to become a good listener, you are helping set your child up to be a fantastic critical thinker. Think back to how many of the steps in critical thinking were contingent upon being a good listener? You need to be able to listen if you want to be able to ensure that you understand the argument being presented to you, therefore listening is crucial to critical thinking, and you need to keep that in mind. This means, then, that teaching your child to be a good listener will encourage your child to be a critical thinker as well.

Luckily, children are usually pretty receptive to learning how to listen. In fact, many may listen on their own, especially if they ask a question that is relevant to you. In order to make sure that your child is a good listener, you want to encourage any time he approaches you and asks for your attention, and teach through example. Your child is going to learn how to be a good listener best if he sees you being a good listener. After all, the most influential teacher that your child will ever have is you.

When you want to teach your child to listen, remember that you need to show good listening skills yourself. Encourage your child to listen by first starting and connecting with your child. Make sure that you are able to relate somehow—point out how you really like what he is doing at that moment and then ask if he can listen to him. You make him feel connected to you when you do this, relating to him, and this means that he is more likely to listen well to you in the first place. This is important—your child learns to be respectful and make sure there is some sort of acknowledged connection between him and the other person when he will be speaking or listening.

Explain things to your child in as clear a manner as possible without dumbing it down. Your child will learn to do this, as well. When you are speaking, you want to do so directly and clearly. Encourage your child to also speak clearly and directly to you when he wants your attention, and respect when he does this, giving him the same attention you are giving him.

You want to make sure that your child's attention is on you when you are speaking to him, and one of the best ways to make this happen is by making sure that you make eye contact when you speak. This also means, however, that you must make eye contact when your child is speaking to you. If you want him to put down the toy when you talk to him, put down your phone when he comes to you. It is only fair and natural for you to respect him the way you expect to be respected as well.

When you do finish speaking to your child, make sure that you always ask if he understands. If he does, ask him to parrot it back to you in his own words to test how well he really does understand it. If he does not understand, encourage him to ask you questions as well, so you can clarify.

When you lead your child by example, you create a child capable of listening well. You put the focus on listening to understand rather than to answer or be obedient, and this is a huge shift in thinking abilities. When your child is able to listen to you and repeat back what you said in different terms, this means that he really hears you, and in really hearing you, he is developing those critical thinking skills.

Positive Mindset Skills and Critical Thinking

One last closely related skill to teaching children critical thinking skills is to encourage positive mindsets. Remember, critical thinking skills involve you being able to parse out those negative biases and mindsets in order to look at the whole picture rather than being dragged down by negative thoughts. This means that you are more likely to be a good critical thinker if you are able to make sure that you can push aside those negative thoughts and encourage positive thoughts to take their place. After all, a massive part of critical thinking is being able to manage the fact that you will fail sometimes—it is a part of the process and only natural. This means then that if you want your child to be skilled and prepared to be a critical thinker, you want to encourage a positive mindset.

When you want to encourage your child to be a positive thinker, perhaps the easiest way to do so is through making sure that your child understands that bad things happen sometimes, but that is okay. If your child messes up his birthday cake, for example, maybe dropping it as it was getting set down on the table, so it turns upside down in the box and no longer looks as fantastic as it did moments prior, you can point out that cake still tastes good, no matter what it looks like, and enjoy it anyway. If your child messes up, you can ask your child what he will do next time that could fix the problem. You are always able to point out what your child has learned, turning it into a positive instead. In doing so, pointing out the positives to focus on instead of the negatives, you can encourage your child to develop the habit of doing the same as well, and that skill will serve him well.

Chapter Three: What are the Benefits of Critical Thinking in Higher Education?

Critical thinking implies acceptance of high standards of excellence and thoughtful command of their applications. An individual can apply these skills to any of life's challenging situations that call for learning, planning, analysis, and reflection. Some of the essential merits of critical thinking in higher education include:

It Encourages Curiosity

Curiosity plays a huge part in learning and exists to help people gain a better understanding of the things that matter and the world at large. This includes the topics students are taught and the ones they find relevant in their daily lives. Students who are critical thinkers remain curious about numerous subjects and usually have a broad interest.

Besides, critical thinkers usually retain curiosity about people and the world and have a deeper appreciation and understanding of different views, beliefs, and cultures. This is part of the reason they tend to become lifelong rs. Besides, since they are naturally curious, they come across tons of opportunities to apply their skills at every moment to any situation. A desire to think critically indicates intent for constructive outcomes, which require them to ask important questions, such as:

a) What is happening?

b) Who is affected, and why is it important?

c) Am I missing anything? If I am, what is it, and why is it important?

d) Where did it come from?

e) How will I know for sure?

f) What can I learn from this?

g) What else should I think about?

h) What if something else happens?

i) Why not?

Critical thinking enables students to be more effective and not take anything at face value. Consequently, they enjoy exploring all sides of a situation, never stop asking pertinent questions, and are always willing to dig deeper to find facts available in all forms of data.

It Boosts Problem-Solving Abilities

People consider critical thinkers to be natural problem-solvers. The ability to solve problem ranks as one of the essential skills students should build upon. Today's students are tomorrow's leaders. As leaders, they will face many challenges and problems; however, they will be able to confidently face any situation or challenge and come up with clever solutions by using their critical thinking skills.

Albert Einstein once confessed that it is not that he is so smart; it is simply that he stays with problems longer. He also said that given an hour to solve a problem, he would likely spend 55 minutes researching and defining it and 5 minutes solving it. This shows a high level of commitment and patience to understand a problem, which is why he is one of history's most respected critical thinkers.

The ability to think critically is essential to becoming an effective problem-solver. Developing this skill prepares students to confidently deal with complex situations that matter to the world they are going to inherit, such as energy crises, global warming, electronic waste management, overpopulation, religious conflicts, political conflicts, water shortages, healthcare needs, pollution, and many more challenges.

Since these complex situations continue to grow and change as the world changes, people must be prepared to face and solve them. These will be those with the ability to think critically to produce creativity and lasting solutions.

It Boosts Creativity

One of the most important skills students need to thrive beyond school is creativity. It ranks second behind problem-solving. Critical thinkers are also creative thinkers. Creativity is an important skill to possess in the modern collaborative workforce. Therefore, critical thinking in professional alliances, marketing, and all aspects of business relies heavily on a person's creativity. When companies get creative with their products and services, and in their marketing campaigns, they often thrive.

Nowadays, every market segment echoes the importance placed on creativity by businesses to increase revenue by improving product and service values. Creative individuals tend to question assumptions and beliefs about many things and do not argue for limitations. Therefore, creativity has limitless potential and is eternal, which suggests that creative individuals are endless. This applies to students of all ages.

It Encompasses a Wide Range of Disciplines

Critical thinking is a multi-faceted practice that has a reputation for cultivating a broad range of cognitive talents in students. Essentially, it is an extra-curricular activity for the mind, which people must frequently exercise to stay healthy, just like a muscle. Some of the cognitive talents and competencies promoted by critical thinking include:

- Evaluative skills

- Decision making

- Reasoning skills

- Questioning skills

- Analytical thinking

- Creative visualization abilities

- Logical thinking

- Open-mindedness

- Planning and organizational skills

- Observational skills

- Self-analysis capacity

- Language skills

This list of skills can easily grow; however, this gives a good idea of what people are enhancing and developing when students learn to think critically in their daily lives.

It is a Skill for Life

Critical thinking is more than a skill for learning, and it is an essential skill for life. According to John Dewey, education is life itself, not a preparation for life. To help students succeed both in school and out of school, educators need to encourage them to develop their critical thinking skills. Critical thinkers are lifelong learners; therefore, if the saying "education is life" is true, then critical thinking is a skill for life.

It Develops Independence

Getting students to start thinking independently is one of the many essential reasons for education. The job of an educator is to empower his or her students to the point where the students do not need him or her anymore. Thinking independently is at the forefront of learning how to be a great or critical thinker and a great leader, as well. This skill teaches students how to make sense of the world based on their observations and personal experiences, and to make smart decisions in the same way.

Consequently, they gain the ability to learn from mistakes and self-confidence as they build productive and successful lives. When students learn to think critically, they tend to think in a self-directed manner. Essentially, they practice a lot of discipline in their thinking, leading to a self-correcting mindset. With time, as they continue to develop their thinking skills through experience and learning, these abilities become second nature.

Therefore, when educators succeed at getting students to think independently, they have given them a valuable gift for life. Critical thinking also gives students the ability to analyze their learning styles, weaknesses, strengths, and encourages them to take ownership and pride in their education.

It Promotes Appropriate Emotional Appeal

Emotions can easily take over when people are arguing their opinions or making critical decisions, especially if they have personal investments in it. However, critical thinking can help people use emotional appeal, allowing their feelings to influence their reasoning, but not control it. For example, a student having a debate on healthcare reform can talk about a loved one who is having trouble with getting insurance, but also support his position with solid evidence from credible sources.

It is the Foundation of a Liberal Democratic Society and Science

For liberal democracy to function properly, it requires citizens and leaders who can think critically about any situation, which will guide their decisions about proper and fair governance and to overcome prejudice and biases. Also, critical thinking is essential in making scientific advancements, especially in the areas of theory and experimentation.

Proof of Success of Critical Thinking to a Student

Students often encounter many assignments and activities in their studies that often demand interpretation and analysis. This requires the application of higher-order thinking skills used to analyze and manipulate information, instead of merely memorizing it. Bloom's thinking triangle provides a useful way of explaining higher-order intellectual domains and learning. Below is a brief description of Bloom's Taxonomy.

Level 1 – Knowledge

Critical thinking improves students' abilities to memorize, recite, and recall most of the facts and information they have learned. Knowledge describes a student's competence and refers to learning information, principles, and concepts regarding certain topics through academic instructions from teachers, books, encyclopedias, media, and other sources. Mostly, it refers to theoretical information acquired about any topic or subject.

The relationship between critical thinking and knowledge is based on a room for improvement. When a student is knowledgeable without critical thinking, he or she can be wrong nor be aware of it, or perhaps, not even care about being wrong. In this modern information and technology age, people keep discovering more knowledge, and this is leading to rapid change in all aspects of life. Therefore, it is essential to develop critical thinking skills to filter this flood of information properly, to purify knowledge, and break it down into facts and informed results.

Students must always keep in mind that combining knowledge with critical thinking will not invalidate their goals, postures, stances, or perspectives. Critical thinking is how to acquire quality from the quantity of knowledge they accumulate from different sources. Some of the information they acquire may be suspect or wrong, but unlike a rotten fruit, wrong information will not spoil valid information.

Once they discover it as being wrong through critical thinking, they can correct their storage of all knowledge. Essentially, the relationship between critical thinking skills and knowledge for students would be in how they use the knowledge they possess.

Level 2 – Comprehension

Comprehension is the ability to understand what one has heard, read, or seen, while critical thinking is the ability to determine whether one should take it as truth or not. These two are closely related, and it would be fair to say students cannot fully comprehend without some level of critical thinking. As educators strive to meet the objectives of their curriculum, they often think about their students' ability to understand. By determining individual skills required for comprehension, they will provide help in critical thinking to develop those skills.

When reading a book, for example, students usually conclude and make inferences to determine what the text in the book is not stating directly. To do this, they must think critically while using specific hints in the text to conclude. For instance, they can infer what is happening when they apply personal experiences to the information presented in the book. Some of the comprehension skills that require critical thinking in education include:

1.   Ability to demonstrate what one has learned

2.   Determining cause and effect

3.   Analyzing characters in literature selections

4.   Interpreting the author's theme or purpose

5.   Debating various issues or topics

In recent years, the study of critical thinking and reading comprehension has received a lot of attention, which is why it has become a popular field in cognitive psychology. Modern academics have developed new theories and trends that offer theoretical models for conceptualizing and explaining reading comprehension by utilizing critical thinking and other related concepts. Both comprehension and critical thinking are essential for students to become great thinkers and achievers.

Level 3 – Application

This is the ability to solve problems and deal with stressful situations by using the acquired information.

An individual can enhance this process significantly by using critical thinking, which is a path to freedom from deception and half-truths. Students have the right to question what they read, hear, and see to get to the truth and apply it to their academic life and beyond. The ability to apply the acquired information is the goal of a liberal education system.

Everyone has heard the stories—the famous movie producer who filed for bankruptcy after gambling his fortune away, or the CEO of a Fortune 500 corporation who lost his job after an affair with his assistant. The list is endless. These individuals, whose talent and brilliance landed them amazing and lucrative jobs, ended up making huge, career-ending, jaw-dropping mistakes when they had everything they could ever need. Well, maybe not everything. They lacked critical thinking skills, which contributed to their downfall.

Numerous studies show that while intelligence can account for certain achievements in life, it does not guarantee future well-being. Critical thinking skills are better predictors of making smart and positive life decisions than smarts. Therefore, students must learn and develop their critical thinking skills to apply the education they have acquired in school more effectively and successfully throughout the rest of their lives.

Schools play an essential role in preparing students for their future by giving them the ability to critically think through situations and problems in effective ways and apply their learning to solve problems and achieve their goals. When it comes to making the smartest choices in school and elsewhere, students must employ critical thinking skills to avoid stress, emotions, or personal prejudices to affect their thinking processes and action plan.

Level 4 – Analysis

Contrary to what many people think, critical thinking and analysis are not the same. Although there are some similarities, there are distinct variances between the two. The process of analysis involves breaking down complex information into basic principles, looking for motives and causes, making assumptions, and finding the evidence to back up one's claims.

Critical thinking, on the other hand, is the process of carefully evaluating situations or information to determine how to interpret it to make the right choice. It involves challenging consensus to come up with innovative solutions and creative ideas. The aim of critical thinking while analyzing something is to find and maintain an objective position. In a classroom situation, when students think critically, they carefully consider all sides of a problem or situation and evaluate its positives and negatives. This helps them make better analyses and improve their creativity.

Analysis and critical thinking are vital aspects of academic life while critical analysis requires students to examine information, evaluate it against what they already know, and determine its validity, critical reflection requires them to examine different ideas to help challenge, justify, or explain what they have experienced in their practice or other people's practice. Literature or theory might give them a different perspective that they should consider or provide evidence to back or challenge their practices or views.

Level 5 – Synthesis

This is the process of putting information together in new or different ways to find and develop a good plan of action or a new solution. Students need critical thinking and reading skills to synthesize better and compare different information and material, identify connections, differences, and similarities, and come up with new ideas and concepts based on interpretations of other arguments or evidence.

Students should think of this process as an extension of analysis or a more sophisticated form of analysis. The main difference between synthesis and analysis is that analysis tends to focus on one source, while synthesis involves several sources. Any scholarly writing or work can include synthesis.

For example, they should consider synthesis existing at both the paragraph and the paper level, such as when writers connect separate pieces of evidence from many sources to back up a paragraph's main idea and develop the paper's thesis statement. It can also take place in the local and global level, such as when writers build a connection across several sections or paragraphs to create a completely new narrative.

Level 6 – Evaluation

This is the topmost cognitive level in Bloom's thinking triangle, and it's referred to as critical evaluation. It is the point where students are required to present and defend their ideas by making value judgments about information, the quality of work done, and the validity of opinions or ideas. Critical thinking is used to think about and evaluate situations or information and reach a positive and helpful conclusion.

In an assignment, students not only need to prove that they have done adequate research and understood the topic in question, but they also need to show that they have seriously thought about the topic and can explain their thinking. In academia, as in all essential areas of life, people need to think critically, analyze and evaluate the information they acquire to make smart decisions and achieve their goals.

Students, especially those in higher education, should not automatically accept everything at face value. A simple Google search for a particular piece of information can generate thousands of purportedly valid information, some of which will be false or misleading.

Therefore, not everything students read is correct, applicable, true, and accurate. Consequently, it is essential for them to collect information from various sources, gather all the evidence, analyze every aspect objectively and rationally, and do it with an open mind to reach their conclusions.

The process of evaluation involves the following:

- Looking at the collected information about a particular topic and identifying the key points, arguments, and assumptions,

- Looking at the issue one needs to address or to solve the problem, and to write it down, and then

- Determining if one will be able to break it down and choose a part or section to start with.

From there, one needs to think about any assumptions one might have about the topic, and why those assumptions exist in one's mind. To decide what information is most appropriate for their purposes, students need to evaluate it carefully and think critically while doing it. They should begin by assessing the sources of the information to ensure they are authoritative and reliable, followed by a careful evaluation of the content itself for evidence of different viewpoints, points of agreement and disagreement, logical connections between different ideas or sources, ideas that are relevant to their needs, and much more.

These days, more than ever before, students need to acquire and develop critical thinking skills, which help to provide a strong foundation for their academic success and success in their future endeavors. Fortunately, an individual can learn and develop these skills. Teaching students these skills is a necessity because they are created to live life and achieve goals.

Critical thinkers are the people that think clearly, objectively and rationally while finding logical connections between ideas. This is a very important skill in exploring and trying to understand the world we live in.

Critical thinking is not all about the gathering of facts, but it is a way of looking at whatever is occupying your mind presently so as to arrive at the best judgment or conclusion. Critical thinkers constantly upgrade or improve their knowledge and take part in self-learning— they make excellent leaders because they are capable of getting to new and high levels of self-improvement as well as self-actualization.

If your aim is to get to your full potential and make a mark in the world, acquire the following characteristics or traits of a critical thinker

Observation

This is one of the first critical thinking skill you learn as a child. It is your ability to see and understand the world around you. A more detailed observation includes the ability to write down details and collect data through senses. Your observations will, in the long run, lead to insight and a better understanding of the world.

Curiosity

This is a very fundamental trait of some of the most successful leaders. Being inquisitive and interested in what is happening around you or the people around you is a trait in many critical thinkers. A curious person does not take anything at face value but will wonder why something is the way it is. Curiosity enables you to be open-minded and directs you to gain more knowledge, which is important for a critical thinker.

Objectivity

Objectivity while looking at information is an important trait in a critical thinker. You must focus on the scientific evaluation and facts of the information you have. When you are an objective thinker, you keep your emotions as well as those of others from affecting or influencing your judgment in any way. However, it is not easy to stay completely objective. We are all influenced by our own viewpoints, perspectives, and experiences in life. In order for you to be objective, you must be aware of your biases and look at issues dispassionately. When you successfully are able to get yourself out of a situation, then you be able to analyze it better.

Introspection

This is the ability to be able to think about how you think or being consciously away from how you think. Introspection is important to critical thinkers to enable them to be aware of their level of attentiveness and alertness of their thoughts as well as their biases. It is the ability to evaluate your deepest and innermost thoughts, sensations and feelings. This ability is closely related to self-reflection that gives you understanding into your mental state and emotions.

Analytical thinking

The best critical thinkers are analytical thinkers, and the best analytical thinkers are the best critical thinkers. In critical thinking, the ability to critically evaluate information on anything or about anything be it a relationship, report or a contract very important. Analysis of information means breaking down information into components and examining how the different parts work separately and together. Analysis depends on observation, collecting and evaluating evidence so as to have an informed conclusion. To be analytical, you must start by being objective.

Identifying biases

Critical thinkers must always challenge themselves to know the evidence that helps form their beliefs and assess the credibility of those sources. When you do this, it will help you question your notions and understand your biases.

Knowing and understanding your biases is important because you become aware of how biases influence your thinking and how the information you have collected may also be skewed. As you collect information, you must ask yourself who stands to benefit from that information, if the source of information biased, and if it omits or overlooks details that don't support its notions or claims.

Determining relevance

Figuring out what information is most relevant, important and meaningful for your consideration is one of the most difficult parts of critical thinking. In many cases, you may be brought for information that seems valuable but may end up being only a small point to consider.

A critical thinker will check if the information is relevant logically to the issue at hand, if it is useful and unbiased or if it is a distraction from a more important point.

Inference

Information most often comes in its raw form. This means that it does not come with a summary that guides you on exactly what it entails. Critical thinkers analyze and draw conclusions and judgment based on raw data. The ability to extrapolate meaning from raw data and discover possible outcomes when evaluating a scenario is what is called inference.

An inference is different from assumptions. For instance, if you find data that says a person weighs 250 pounds, you can assume they are overweight. However, you may come across other data that points out the person is well within their recommended weight because of their height and body composition.

Compassion and empathy

Compassion and empathy may seem as negative traits for critical thinkers because they are emotional traits that can influence the situation or its outcome. However, the reason for having compassion is to have concern for others and value their welfare. Lack of compassion will make you view every situation and information from the point of cold data and scientific facts. Looking at situations without compassion may make it easy to allow your cynicism to be toxic and become suspicious of every information you have. A good critical thinker takes into account the human element in situations because everything you do is not about detached information or data.

Humility

This is the ability to acknowledge your own shortcomings and see the positive attributes of others objectively and accurately. Humility enables you to be aware of your weaknesses as well as your strengths. For critical thinkers, humility is a very important element that helps them to be able to stretch and be open-minded. With intellectual humility, you are open-minded about other people's viewpoints, acknowledge when wrong, and are flexible to change your beliefs when called upon to.

Willingness to change the status quo

In business, critical thinking means questioning business practices that have long been established and refusing to conform to traditional methods with the excuse that it is how things have always been done. Critical thinkers are in search of thoughtful and smart methods and answers that include every relevant practice and information available. Challenging the status quo may not be viewed favorably, but a creative and innovative mind is an integral part of a critical thinker.

Open-mindedness

This is the ability of a critical thinker to be able to step back from a situation and see a broader view without being attached to the situation. Critical thinkers do not take sides or jump into conclusions. They are open-minded in how they approach a situation and are able to embrace the viewpoints of others.

Aware of common thinking errors

A critical thinker will never allow logic and reasoning to be tainted by illusions and misconceptions. They are consciously aware of logical fallacies which are mistakes in reasoning that find their way into debates and arguments. Some of the common fallacies in thinking are:

- Circular reasoning where the start of the argument or its conclusion is used to support the same argument.

- Cognitive shortcut bias is where you refuse to change from a favored argument or view regardless of the availability of other possibilities that are more effective.

Confusing correlation with causation is where you assume that when two things happen together, one must be the cause for the other even without evidence. This assumption is not justified.

Creative thinking

Critical thinkers are also creative thinkers. Creative thinkers reject problem-solving in a standardized manner and prefer to think outside the box. They have many interests and multiple viewpoints to a problem. They are also open-minded and like to experiment with different methods when solving a problem.

The difference between creative thinkers and critical thinkers is that creative thinkers generate a lot of ideas while critical thinkers analyze and evaluate the ideas. Creativity is important as it brings a variety of ideas while critical thinking will focus on the ideas and analyze them in order to pick the best idea to solve a problem or to draw conclusions on.

Effective communicators

Effective communication is characterized by a clear thought process. Most problems in communication are based upon an inability to critically think through a situation or see it through varied viewpoints. Critical thinking is the tool we use to build our thoughts and express them coherently. A good critical thinker must be able to communicate their ideas in a convincing way and internalize the responses of others.

Active listeners

To be a good critical thinker, you must be a good active listener. Critical thinkers engage in active listening because they also use other people's viewpoints to form conclusions. They participate in a conversation and avoid being passive. They ask questions in order to avoid assumptions, they collect information and seek to gain knowledge by asking open-ended questions that enable them to dig deeper into the issue.

Chapter Five: Quick Thinking Exercises to Boost Critical Thinking Skills

Exercise 1: Improve Comedy

This may seem intimidating, especially if you are afraid of public speaking, but by putting yourself on the spot in a situation like improve comedy, you are encouraging yourself to have to work on your thinking on your feet skills. This means that you will have no choice but to think quickly about subjects that you may not have considered before. This means that your mind has to get good at figuring out what is the best possible progression quickly, in a lighthearted, low-stakes situation.

If you cannot find an improve comedy venue around you, you could try setting up something similar at home with some trusted friends. Put out a bunch of different random topics, or use a deck of cards with several topics written on them, and have them drawn at random. You are then required to talk about the subject for three minutes and make the group laugh as much as possible. The group then has to score your performance, or you can have a judge that is not playing that does all of the grading.

This is going to be difficult, especially at first, if you are shy, but you are learning to think on your feet, which can really help you begin to think critically quickly by exercising your mind. After all, your mind needs to be exercised just as much as your body does, and this is a fun way to do so.

Exercise 2: Get into a Debate

You could try finding a local debate team or just meeting up with one of your friends that loves to argue. When you debate with someone, you are forced to think quickly and come up with counter-arguments quickly in order to protect your own arguments. This is great for critical thinking since it already uses logic and arguments, and you are also thinking quickly at the same time. Thinking quickly is crucial to being a critical thinker since you need to be able to figure out important details quickly and easily.

When you do this, however, it is strongly recommended that you try to avoid topics that you know are likely to get heated, such as hot-topic politics. However, if you keep it light, with topics such as defending or arguing why a movie was not that great, or why a certain restaurant is far superior to another, you can keep the argument itself low-stress without ruining relationships while still making sure that you are able to practice crucial skills.

You could even set this up to be a weekly arrangement, encouraging you and your friend to come up with a new topic and meet at a new location every time. The practice will be good for you, and in actually organizing everything to be formal, you will find that you greatly benefit everyone involved.

Exercise 3: Play Quick-Thinking Board Games

Games that are designed to make you think, such as quick trivia games designed to be answered immediately as soon as you can press the button or buzzer can be a great way to speed up your quick-thinking skills. You may even choose to race a game show on television in coming up with answers as quickly as possible in order to help you exercise your mind.

Ultimately, much of learning to speed up your own mind is done through sheer repetition. The more you are able to exercise your mind, the more likely it is to begin to think quicker. Doing so can help you become a far more efficient critical thinker as well, thanks to the fact that when you are able to begin drawing information quickly, you will be able to do so in a wider range quicker as well. After all, thinking on your feet is a skill that can be developed just as much as other skills that are important to critical thinking.

Exercise 4: Timed Writing Sprints

Thinking quickly does not only have to only involve your mind. You can also speed up other skills as well while also practicing your quick thinking. For example, you can do timed writing sprints. When you do this, you are going to be making it a point to write as much as you can about a new subject every single day. If you cannot write well or effectively, or you do not necessarily care about your typing ability, instead, try using a pencil and quickly jotting down as much as you possibly can.

Every day, find a new subject at random—you could use a random page online, such as the *I'm feeling lucky* search option on Google or some other method, and then write about whatever the result is for three minutes. You need to brainstorm as much as you can in those three minutes in order to figure out everything that you possibly know about the topic. If you write about it, you may consider extending your writing time out to more than 10 minutes. In doing so, you are encouraging your mind to access a random set of information essentially on-demand and then processing it as quickly as possible to come up with as much information as you possibly could on the subject. Doing so regularly will not only help your writing speed, either by pen or via typing, but it will also help you learn to up your speeds when it comes to brainstorming as well.

Creative Thinking Exercises to Boost Critical Thinking Skills

Exercise 1: Alternative Solution Methods

Identify a problem that you are having or had recently and think about the solution that is being used. Can you come up with another way of fixing the problem that you had not originally thought about? Doing so can really help you figure out how to exercise your creative thinking skills. Effectively, what you want to do is figure out how to think outside the box about a problem that you are currently facing or that you have recently faced.

Since several issues can be difficult to solve, if you do not know what you are doing, sometimes you have no choice but to look at things in a creative manner. This means that you may need to look at things from all sides to really understand the best way to progress. Even if you may already have a perfectly viable solution, is there another one that would also work? Why would it work? Exploring other options helps you become flexible in your thinking. You get to a point where you are able to address issues with ease because you are used to working in unconventional methods. When the unconventional solutions become easy to come up with and configure, you may find that conventional methods become easier as well.

Exercise 2: Consider the Opposite Position

Find an argument that you have made in the past or a cause that you are truly passionate about. Now, you are going to have to turn that position upside down altogether. You may need to do some research in order to figure out how best to turn the position around and take the other one, but it will teach you to think creatively. You will have to begin considering perspectives that you may not have otherwise considered, and in doing so, you can start to figure out how best to become a flexible thinker.

This is probably one of the more difficult exercises, as you will be challenged to come up with an argument that is truly the opposite of any that you would truly believe, and you need to actually support it. However, it also benefits you to begin looking at situations in ways that are going to welcome diversity as well, making it doubly useful when it comes to developing critical thinking skills. Even though you may feel like this is an exercise that you would hate, you may find it to be incredibly useful to you in the future, especially after trying it out a few times.

Exercise 3: Catastrophic Problem Prompt

Imagine that you wake up one morning to find that you are not at home anymore—you are lost in a cave with no idea where you are or how to get back to where you belong. When you walk around, you see all sorts of strange, foreign creatures and naturally believe that you are dreaming. However, several pinches confirm that you can, in fact, feel your body around you and that you are not asleep. Around you, you find a short man covered in hair that stands at your knee and is holding a helmet, a small dragon that is incredibly snarky, and a tall woman who does not seem to speak English at all. How do you figure out where you are and find your way home?

Turn the above prompt into a writing challenge in which you figure out how to get out of this sudden, unexpected situation. You will be working on your creative thinking skills while also using critical thinking skills, such as problem-solving. Writing may not be your thing or something you care for at all, but it can be incredibly useful when you are attempting to practice your critical thinking skills. When you write a story prompt, such as the above one, you are stuck figuring out how to solve problems that are impossible in real life. Because these problems are entirely impossible in real life, you never would have considered them. Now, in forcing yourself to write about it, you are attempting to come up with a logical way out of an impossible situation with only the information that has been provided to you. As a bonus, you may develop a nice hobby in writing if you happen to love the process!

Exercise 4: Try a Roleplaying Game

Yes, this may seem counterintuitive, but playing video games can actually help you figure out how to think critically. Despite the common misconception that video games may melt the brains of children, they actually do encourage a wide range of important benefits, such as hand-eye coordination and encouraging cooperation and problem-solving. RPGs, in particular, are notorious for having all sorts of ridiculous puzzles that may require some critical and creative thinking skills.

The RPG you play is not quite as important as you actually dedicate yourself to doing so in the first place. Several are paced, so beginners can pick them up if you have never played before. If you are not new to games, you can use this as an excuse to pick up the game and practice—call it your critical thinking training and enjoy! This is an enjoyable way to get in that practice that also makes your work seem like play—because it is! When you play through these games, you will encounter all sorts of puzzles, to varying extents and difficulties.

Keep in mind that you may need to scale up or down the difficulty level for yourself.

Analytical Thinking Exercises to Boost Critical Thinking Skills

Exercise 1: Brain Games

Brain games are a fantastic way for you to boost your analytical thinking abilities without having to bore yourself while doing so. There are several games out there that will boost your analytical skills and improve your ability to think critically. These games, from Sudoku to other sorts of word puzzles in which you must unscramble words, can help you figure out how best to think analytically about a situation around you, and you do not even need to go out of your way to find them, either.

If you are reading this, you probably have access to the internet on some sort of device. The internet holds a plethora of information just waiting for you to take advantage of it, and this includes several apps that are designed to help you develop your ability to think analytically. You can download several apps that can help you with this analytical thinking and spend just 10 minutes a day exercising your brain. As you do so, your capacity for analytical thinking will increase. Remember, your brain needs to be exercised just as much as your body, and this is a great way to do so. If you prefer numbers over word games, you could play a game such as Sudoku. If you prefer a word or story game, you could focus on games that are designed around you, solving a mystery.

Exercise 2: Escape Rooms

Yet another way to make this process fun, escape rooms can be a great exercise in ensuring that you strengthen your analytical skills. If you do not know what an escape room is, they are rooms or buildings designed to be like a game—you are locked in for a specific amount of time with no escape, and you have a determined amount of time to solve the puzzle to escape. Along the way, you and a group of people will find all sorts of clues that point you one direction or another, and it will be on you to figure out how best to get through.

These rooms are not particularly easy, though they are fun for those who like games and challenges. You will have to figure out the clues, decipher them, and follow their lead while under the pressure of the clock. However, they are quite enjoyable despite the intense pressure, and if this is your idea of a good time, you can gather up a group of friends and go have fun regularly. Of course, these rooms are not always available, depending on your location. Keep in mind that you may need to travel or may not be able to find one. If you can, however, this is a great and fun way to build up those analytical skills, while possibly having a date night at the same time!

Exercise 3: 10 Minute Learning Period

Every day, challenge yourself to learn something new. Whatever you choose, make sure you spend 10 minutes learning as much as possible about it in order to really help your mind absorb information. Part of being able to analyze comes in the form of being able to also rationalize information quickly and effectively, and sometimes, the best way to do so is through choosing a topic at random and learning as much as you can about it.

Think about it this way—if you have ten minutes to learn everything you need to know about aquariums and how to keep them, what are you going to look at? You need to be able to analyze the information that you know about aquariums already to figure out where your energy is best served. If you do not know the difference between tropical, cold water, and saltwater fish, you are probably not going to spend the entire ten minutes reading about the benefits to the different shapes of tanks and whether you want acrylic, glass, or something else—you would probably look for a beginner's guide that would tell you all of the relevant information and start broadly. In starting as broadly as possible, you are able to get the general idea down before you start specializing. After all, knowing the difference between acrylic and a glass tank is not going to help you keep a fish alive.

Exercise 4: Try a New Project

Every now and then, when you have the time to properly invest, try something new. It is good for you to try new things once and a while to break up the monotony of day to day life, but you can also find serious benefits in teaching yourself a new skill suddenly. For example, if you know that you need to be able to multitask, but you have always struggled with it, try learning how to cook a meal that requires plenty of multitasking. You can start with something a bit easier that requires you to cook and prepare two different foods at once, for example, and slowly work your way up.

In choosing a new skill that is something you have little or no experience in, you are forcing your mind to accommodate. You have no choice but to learn the information as quickly as possible, which will force your mind into analysis mode. You will be able to make sure that your mind is focusing on how to get through the skill you have picked up, learning the important information first, which encourages the analysis of information.

Chapter Six: Practical Examples That Help To Improve Communication Skills, Self-Confidence, and Problem Solving

Have you ever heard the quote, "The biggest room in the world is the room for improvement" by Helmut Schmidt? With application to critical thinking and sound reasoning, everyone has his or her role to play in improving communication skills, self-confidence, and problem-solving skills. Therefore, here is a list of tips you can apply in everyday situations with the foundation of critical thinking.

Practical Examples that Help an Individual to Improve Communication Skills

Watch Your Body Language

When conversing with people, your body language can send the right or the wrong message. For example, if you tell someone you are listening, but your eyes are staring at your phone, then your body language is communicating something different from what your mouth is saying. To improve your communication, you need to watch your body language, maintain eye contact, express positive facial expressions, and relax your posture.

Practice

If you want to improve your communication skills, you need to practice a lot. Start by practicing on friends and family, and then ask them for honest feedback. Feedback helps you know your weak points and improve. For example, if they tell you, you are not audible, or your conversations are making them uncomfortable, then you know that next time, you'll be clear and audible, and avoid specific topics.

Tailor Your Communication Skills to the Audience

Your communication skills are not one size fits all; one style will not work in all instances. It is essential to tailor your communication skills to your current audience. If you are communicating with kids, the use of gestures, pitch, and tone variations, and adding props will work very well, but this would not be ideal when communicating with the board.

Listening skills

Having good listening skills is half the equation of being an excellent communicator. You need to listen to others actively. It is essential to learn how to pay attention to people when they speak to you. When you listen, you allow the other person to express himself or herself, and at the same time, it shows you respect them. Avoid a situation where phones or people around you are distracting you.

Empathy

An excellent way to improve your communication skills is to empathize with others. This involves connecting with others emotionally. Learn how to understand other people's emotions and respond appropriately. For example, when someone is shouting because of anger, empathizing with them can help diffuse their emotions.

Practical examples that Help an Individual to Improve Self-confidence

Be More Positive

Therefore, to boost your self-confidence, it is vital to turn your negative thoughts into positive ones. Do not dwell too much on things that make you feel bad about yourself, because these will arguably add no value in any area of your life. For example, if you surround yourself with friends who are mean and put you down all the time, avoid them, and cut off them off from your life because they will pull you back and never add value to your life. Find people who make you feel good about yourself because these will have the exact opposite effect and build you up.

Take Care of Yourself

Another way to boost your self-confidence is to take care of your body and your mind. Exercising, eating healthy, and sleeping well are sure ways of boosting your confidence because they not only make you feel good and refreshed, but they also contribute to your overall fitness and outward appeal. When you exercise, your body also releases endorphins hormones, which make you feel good and look great.

Avoid Comparison

Comparing yourself to others is a sure way to decrease your self-confidence because that is a sign of envy, and no two people, including twins, will be the same in every way. Life is not a competition; everyone is running his or her race because we all possess different gifts and abilities, suitable to help us live out our lives in the best way. Stop comparing your wealth, body, skills, and even families to others. Learn to run your race and pat yourself on the back when you achieve a milestone.

Erase Self-doubt

Sometimes we put things off until we feel confident enough, but sometimes doing those things is the best way to gain confidence. Invite that friend out on a date and plan that wedding. Instead of putting things off, prepare, and practice to boost morale when you get to do them. Sometimes facing your fears is all you need to increase your self-confidence because one more victory will surely give you the motivation to try new things.

Don't Be Too Hard On Yourself

Sometimes a little tender, love, and care are all you need. Do not beat yourself up when you make a mistake; cut yourself some slack because everyone falls short sometimes, and if that were never the case, life would not be so exciting. You should find comfort in the fact that no one is perfect, and there will never be a perfect human being. If you fail at something, aim at improving next time and avoid dwelling on it too much. Only focus on the things you can change

Practical Examples that Help an Individual to Improve Problem-solving

Engage Your Brain

To improve your problem-solving skills, engage your brain with puzzles and games. Play games like Sudoku, chess, board games, or the Rubik's cube. Sometimes an individual can use the strategies he or she uses to win these games in real-life situations and help build his or her problem-solving skill. The brain is a fantastic organ that becomes even more useful when it is busy doing something exciting and challenging for specific periods.

Use a Step-By-Step Cycle

When you are solving a problem, follow a simple step-by-step process to get a solution, since trying to solve everything at once will prove to be frustrating. One, identify and understand the problem, two, gather any useful information, three, find methods to solve it and assess the pros and cons of each approach, four, choose the best method to solve the problem. Lastly, evaluate your result; did it solve the problem? If not, go back to step one. This approach will give you the privilege of small victories that will motivate you to complete the overall challenge.

Change Your Mindset

If you always think things are too hard to solve, change that mindset because if you do not, they will eventually turn out harder than they need to be. View that problem as a chance to grow and find a solution, or a stepping-stone towards something more significant. Be open-minded; this also reduces your chances of being stressed when you have a problem. In reality, you are sure to encounter problems, but with the right mindset, you will overcome them. The sooner you come to terms with how to solve them, the better for you.

Focus on the Solution

Sometimes we tend to focus on the problem as opposed to focusing on the solution. When you focus on the problem, you will fill yourself with negativity, which counters your ability to look for solutions. For example, when you notice you always arrive too late to work, it is easy to blame it on traffic or use of public transportation and leave it at that, because there is arguably nothing you can do to improve the transport industry. However, you can choose to look at the whole issue of getting to work late from a solution point of view. Maybe you get late because you sleep late and snooze the alarm in the morning and, in turn, end up leaving late for work. As a solution, you can decide to start sleeping early, which will contribute to your waking up on time, and consequently lead you to get to work on time.

Critical thinking is an important skill for the modern times. It is about analyzing, questioning and challenging situations as well as issues and information of all types. We use critical thinking skills when we ask questions about theories, conventional wisdom, survey results among others. So what strategies should we use to build these skills in students? The following techniques help students acquire critical thinking skills and have a great impact on their learning.

1) Socratic seminars – these are wonderful tools that facilitate in-depth conversations between students based on a given text. A teacher usually assigns a text to students and asks them to read and prepare for a class discussion. The students discuss amongst themselves, listening to each other with each student participating. The teacher acts as the moderator of the discussion and remains neutral.

2) Simulations – simulations are a great way to encourage critical thinking. Some areas of study come to life as students make decisions as though they are

experiencing events first hand. Simulations usually provide a lasting impact on the retention of content.

3) Encourage creativity – instead of giving detailed instructions or directions to students to complete an activity, just make materials required available and step back and let the children use their creativity. It may surprise a teacher how much students can accomplish if left alone to control their own learning.

4) Depth and complexity icons – the in-depth complexity icons that were introduced by Sandra Kaplan that include ethics, details, unanswered questions, trends, rules, languages, big ideas, and disciplines help stimulate in-depth analysis. When used across various levels, they help students think about a subject critically.

5) Compare and Contrast – encourage students to compare and contrast ideas and concepts, theories, objects, and living things. Comparison charts can help in this exercise.

6) Literature circles – allow students to select books that they can present and discuss in the classroom. When they discuss amongst themselves, students get motivated

to dig deeper and critically think about issues presented in the book that on their own they may not have considered.

7) Debates – debates are known to sharpen students' ability or persuasion skills. They are able to persuade a given audience about a particular topic and to do this they need to analyze the information they have on the particular subject critically. Debates also help students to listen and speak articulately of their points actively as well as enhance their critical thinking skills.

8) Instant challenges – this is an excellent way to begin the day in school because the students are forced to think critically and express creativity under pressure. Students work as a team or in groups, complete a given challenge within a short time, and then do a presentation of their work to the class that will judge their performance. This is also a great way to develop and even improve critical thinking skills in students.

9) Open-ended questioning – many students are used to questions that offer only one answer. Give students open-ended questions that will enable them to think at a

higher level and will trigger their curiosity to learn more and critically analyze every information they find.

10) Reciprocal Teaching – divide students into small groups with each having a role as a question generator, clarifier, summarizer, or predictor. They can also take turns as moderator. The aim of reciprocal teaching is to encourage students to get involved in the discussion and deeply think about what they are reading.

How to Teach Critical Thinking in Schools

Critical thinking skills are important skills in our day-to-day lives. Critical thinking skills are important to students too. There are many ways in which a teacher can seek to teach these skills to the students. Critical thinking is not only about clear and rational thinking, but it also involves independent thinking. This means formulating opinions and coming up with unbiased conclusions based on the available information. It calls for discipline in analysis and identifying connections between ideas as well as being open to wide viewpoints and opinions.

To teach critical thinking skills does not require special equipment but rather curious minds with simple strategies.

The following techniques will help a teacher in teaching critical thinking skills to students:

Begin with questions

This is the simplest way to start critical thinking lessons. Whatever you want to explore and discuss should not be in the form of questions that require a 'yes'' or 'no' answer. Develop essential questions that create the curiosity for knowledge and problem-solving. When you pose these questions, encourage the students to brainstorm as you list possible answers on the board. Having this kind of an open discussion with students is a great way to collectively identify the problem, analyze the information, and come up with the best solution.

Create a foundation

Information is central to any critical thinking exercise. Begin critical thinking exercises with a review of relevant information. This ensures that they are able to

91

remember facts on the topic in discussion. These may come from:

- Reading assignments or home works

- Critical thinking exercises

- A text reading or video

Consult the classics

Challenging narratives from great literary works are a perfect way to start critical thinking. Use these works for lessons in plot predictions, motivation, or themes. You can explore things like

- Critical thinking and Shakespeare

- The critical thinking community among others.

Creating a country

This can be a great learning project needing sufficient research to discover what makes a country, and in the process, the students get to learn history, politics, geography, and many more. Leave the assignment as an open-ended exercise for a few days and see what the students come up with.

Use information fluency

Critical thinking as a tool enables you to know when to pursue or discard information. Students must understand how to collect the appropriate information to inform their thinking. Understanding information fluency is key to teaching critical thinking skills to students. Students need to master the correct use of information in order to succeed in their school life. It is about developing the skills to dig through knowledge and finding the most appropriate and useful facts to enable problem-solving.

Utilize peer groups

Because of digitalization, many students excel in environments where critical thinking skills are developed through collaboration and teamwork. Show the students how their peers are excellent sources of knowledge, problem-solving techniques, and questions.

Try one sentence

This technique involves an exercise where students are divided into small groups of 5 to 7 students. Next, the students are each instructed to write one sentence describing a topic then the paper is passed to the next student that adds their interpretation of the next step in one sentence but folds down the paper to cover their sentence and so forth. Each time the paper is passed on, the student can only see one sentence. This exercise aims at teaching the students to close in on a specific moment. They also get to learn how to apply knowledge and logic in explaining themselves as much as possible.

Problem-solving

This is the best way of teaching critical thinking skills to students. Assign a problem that is open-ended to allow the students to explore and analyze knowledge through critical thinking.

Return to roleplaying

This is an excellent way of practicing critical thinking. When actors are given a character to play, they do a lot of research into the character because the role involves taking the persona of the character—hence calling for both creative and analytical mind. Pair students up and assign them to research on a conflict that involves interaction between historical figures. Help them decide what character they will each play—they each have varying points of view on the conflict. Let them analyze it until they can each explain the other's point of view then suggest a compromise.

Speaking with sketch

In as much as we are visual learners, it can be challenging to communicate an idea effectively without words. However, the translation of thoughts to picture encourages critical thinking. It guides children using varied mental skill set and for them to get totally invested in the idea.

Prioritize it

Every subject presents critical thinking opportunities. Prioritize critical thinking skills in your lessons. Check for understanding and create room for discussion. This practice will start cultivating critical thinking as a way of learning rather than an activity.

Change their misconceptions

A lot of work and concentration is involved in critical thinking, but it is best to let students do the process by themselves. However, it can be helpful to step in and help where necessary in order to correct misconceptions or assumptions. Students will richly benefit from critical thinking for better learning in the long run.

There are many techniques that a person can apply to acquire and develop critical thinking skills. Different disciplines may apply different methods, but in all disciplines, the critical thinking process must be applied. Once you understand the process, you can formulate your own ways of acquiring or improving critical thinking as long as you apply the processes. Always remember that the skills of critical thinking are acquired over a period of time through practice.

Chapter Eight: Obstacles to Creative Thinking and Overcoming Them

Ever felt like your mind is not working, like you can't solve a basic problem? There are several obstacles to creative thinking that may be obstructing you from improving your problem-solving skills. In order to overcome them, you must first recognize them. Some of these obstacles include:

1)_Lack of Direction from Others and Yourself

Lack of clearly defined goals and objectives is the first obstacle to critical thinking. Your goals and objectives must be clearly written down together with detailed plans of action. When you are completely clear about what you need and the way to go about it, your creative mind becomes alive. You immediately start generating ideas and insights that help you improve your critical thinking skills.

2)_Being Afraid of Failure

Fear of failure or loss is the second obstacle to creative thinking. Many people are afraid of being wrong or making mistakes and even losing money or time. The anticipation and possibility of failure paralyze action and becomes a major reason for ineffective problem solving and failure. Build confidence is using the skill of critical analysis where you are sure that the information you have will lead to an informed conclusion.

3)_Being Afraid of Rejection

The fear of criticism, rejection, ridicule or scorn is the third major obstacle to critical thinking. The fear of sounding stupid or looking foolish makes one backtrack on critically thinking through. This is as a result of the desire to feel approved, liked and so forth even by people you don't know. You decide because you want to get along, you then must go along with their findings. Many people live lives of mediocrity or underachievement because they are afraid to be judged or rejected; hence, they cannot bring themselves to sell their ideas. Because of this fear, they play safe and settle for far less than they believe in.

4)_Never Changing or Adapting to the Situation

Homeostasis is the subconscious desire to stay and remain consistent with the things you have said or done in the past. This is a major obstacle in critical thinking. This impulse holds a person back from achieving success. You find comfort in doing what you have always done, and you get stuck. All progress stops, and you start rationalizing why you are not changing. Homeostasis is a major killer to critical thinking and creative thinking.

5)_Not Thinking Proactively

Another obstacle to critical thinking is passivity. If you decide not to stimulate your mind with new information and ideas, it loses its energy and vitality. Instead of thinking critically, proactively and creatively continuously, you become automatic and passive in your thinking. Routine is a major cause of passive thinking. When you follow the same routine every day in doing things, your mind is never challenged to find new ways of doing things. When you don't challenge your mind, it becomes complacent and dull. If a person proposes a new way of doing things, you will react with discouragement and negativity, and you start feeling threatened by any suggestion of change.

6)_You Rationalize and Never Improve

Rationalizing is another major obstacle to creative thinking. As rational creatures, we always use our minds to explain the world to ourselves in order to feel more secure and understand it better. This means you always come up with quick explanations as to why you have done or not done something. When you constantly rationalize what you decide, you will not improve your performance.

For instance, as an entrepreneur, there are two main reasons why critical thinking is important to you. The first one is problem-solving and decision-making. At least more than 50% of your time as an entrepreneur is spent solving problems. Becoming a critical thinker as well as a creative thinker will help you in your day-to-day problem-solving abilities that will be inevitable. These skills will enable you to become more successful in your business.

Secondly, we all want to make more money. Your problem-solving abilities are also important in determining how much money you will make.

There are seven habits that form the mindset of a critical thinker at all times. These habits include:

- Truth-seeking – a critical thinker has intellectual integrity and a desire to strive for the best and factual knowledge as much as possible.

- Open-minded – a critical thinker has a tolerant mindset to divergent views and sensitive to their own biases.

- Analytical – a critical thinker's mind is habitually alert and vigilant to potential problems and consequences that may be short-term or long-term as a result of decisions made or actions taken.

- Systematic – the mindset of a critical thinker is that of organization and order in their approach to solving problems. They are persistent, orderly, focused and diligent.

- Confident in reasoning – their mindset is that of truthfulness in their own reasoning skills in order to yield good judgment.

- Inquisitive – their mindset is that of learning. They habitually strive to be informed; they are naturally curious about how things work and seeking new information every day.

- Judicious – a critical thinker has cognitive maturity and realizes all questions are not as they seem, nothing is black or white, and judgment may sometimes be made in the context of uncertainty.

Here, you have learned why critical thinking is different from ordinary thinking and how it is much more advantageous to approach issues or problems from the point of critical thinking in order to get the best conclusions. Look at the characters of a critical thinker and try to develop the same characters in your thinking. Then, see how much better problem solving will become for you!

Chapter Nine: Critical Thinking for Better Decision Making

To achieve a goal or an objective, you need to possess decision-making skills. As we have seen, decision-making revolves around making choices and solving problems. This often requires brainstorming and finding out the why, what, when, where, and how as a way to overcome any obstacles that manifest in the course of finding solutions.

Decision-making starts with thinking and then finding out the best way to transform the thoughts into action. Below are some strategies you can employ to improve your decision making skills.

Why Decision Making is Important

Decision making is important because everything that happens to you starts with a decision. The relationships that you choose to form, the job that you choose to work at, and even what day you go to the grocery store are all results of decisions that you have made. As you learn to think critically, you will find that your decision making becomes easier. Rather than reacting based on your emotions or irrational thought, you can make the decisions that will lead to happiness, success and the achievement of your goals.

Don't Try to Be a Perfectionist

Stop trying to be a perfectionist. There is nothing wrong with wanting to do your best. However, you need to know when it is the right time to stop. It doesn't mean that you should settle for less if it isn't the best. It simply means that you should set criteria and stick to it. A perfectionist hesitates while taking the first step and this can be a significant deterrent when it comes to decision-making. A perfectionist always believes that there are only two possible outcomes in any given situation, either success or failure. This isn't how the world works. It is great that you want to be good at something, but it is equally important to understand where to draw the line as well. Don't think that a task isn't completed just because it isn't perfect. Also, this mentality can prevent you from starting something. Not just starting, but even finishing it as well. Instead of chasing perfection, you should focus on being better and completing the task.

Determine Important Factors First

Have you ever wondered how two people can look at the same situation and come to different conclusions? People develop unique perspectives and conclusions because of their core values and what matters most to them during the decision-making process. This is the reason that you must make your own decisions nobody else can decide what decisions will meet your core values and resonate with your life. Before decision making, create a list of the things most important to you.

Think When Your Mind is Clear

Have you ever agreed to something or been persuaded easier because you were tired? You may not have had the energy or motivation to argue your point or come up with a rebuttal. This is a common occurrence. The research shows that when you do not get enough sleep, it affects your ability to make rational decisions. This is especially true in stressful situations. To keep your mind clear, try to make your decisions after you've had some rest. There must be some truth to the common phrase 'sleep on it' after all.

When thinking critically about a decision, timing is everything. While you may not have unlimited time for weighing your options, particularly in times of stress or when making business situations, timing drastically affects the critical thinking process.

Timing determines how long you have to gather information and broaden your perspective before diving into the decision-making process. It determines how quickly you must analyze information and look for links between the facts of the current situation and what you already know. Timing also affects the amount of pressure that you feel, which may result in a decision based on pressure rather than one that fulfills the goal of creating the best-case scenario.

Situations will arise where you have to decide based on the limited information that you have. Know all the driving factors in these decisions and be sure that the choice you make comes from a sound place of mind, rather than one that is frazzled with the pressure of making a quick decision.

Listen to Your Gut

We all have an inner voice that tries helping us in deciding what is right and wrong. However, more often than not, we tend to ignore this inner voice. We ignore it so much that it starts becoming feeble. We are all born with an instinctual compass that can help us determine what the best course of action is for us. This compass is your conscience. Whenever you think you are doing something wrong, don't you feel a sinking sensation in your gut that tells you that something is amiss? Learn to listen to your gut. If you have a bad feeling about something, then it probably is bad. Your intuition can guide you through a difficult decision; just learn to listen to it. In our process of growing up, we often tend to ignore our intuition because of what others say and do.

Understanding Cognitive Biases

Perhaps one of the most clichéd questions that a therapist will ask their patient is "tell me more about your childhood." Human beings collect their experiences. Depending on whether a particular incident or situation is positive or negative, our minds start creating biases. For instance, if you were ever mugged on a specific street, it is very likely that you will try to avoid that street in the future. Or perhaps you were in a relationship with an unfaithful partner and this will create trust issues and will make you question how faithful any potential partner is. These are instances of negative cognitive bias that your brain develops. Such biases can have a lasting impact on your ability to decide. In the same sense, your brain can favor certain things just because of the positive experience you might have had while growing up. Bias can impair your sense of decision-making and prevent you from thinking rationally.

Choosing your Timing Wisely

You should be mindful of the time when you are deciding as well. For instance, it isn't advisable that you make a big decision after an argument with your partner. This is bound to affect your ability to think clearly, and you will end up doing something impulsively. We often tend to make decisions when we aren't in the right frame of mind. When you are feeling angry, it is likely that you will end up doing something rashly without thinking things through and without thinking about the repercussions of your actions. Always make decisions when your mind isn't foggy. However, spending too much time thinking or overanalyzing is a dangerous thing as well. When in a bad mood, don't make a quick decision. Sleep on it or spend some time to think it through.

Maximize Instead of Settling

Many people go with the decision that is 'good enough' rather than making a decision that will fulfill all their needs. Maximization is about not settling for what works. It is about looking for the best solution rather than settling for a decision. When we make decisions, it can be easy to limit ourselves to just two or three choices. The reality is that three are unlimited possibilities. If you cannot choose because you are unsure of which option will be best, try to find a solution that creates the important benefits from each of the plausible solutions.

Decide on Things That Are Important

Regardless of your age or profession, you will be faced with numerous decisions every day. However, not every decision needs to be given the same weight. For instance, having to decide the theme for a project needs to be given more weight than the choosing what you should have for your next meal. Learn to differentiate between the decisions that are important and the ones that aren't. You obviously shouldn't spend the same amount of time trying to research about a particular lawn fertilizer when compared to learning about a specific health condition. Learn to prioritize your tasks and spend more time while deciding something of significance. When you learn to prioritize your ability to make decisions, you can divert most of your energy towards things that are worth something.

Predicting the Outcome

Sometimes, it is not until after making a decision that you recognize all the real-life consequences. This is especially true of rash decisions made in the heat of the moment or without rational thought. Rather than worrying about the consequences later, think about the outcomes of each for each of your options before making the final decision.

As you consider the outcome, it is important to remember that every action you take has an outward ripple. Even something that seems simple, like walking your dog to the park, affects the people that you bump into on the sidewalk and the other pets in the park. It influences the people driving cars that have to stop for you to cross the road.

As you consider the outcome of your decision, think about how it will affect you personally. Then, consider how it will affect everyone else around you. Be sure to think of the short-term and long-term results of your choice and what obstacles might arise as a result of your decision.

There are some who are naturally good decision makers, some who like surrounding themselves with good decision makers, and others who aren't that good at it. Well, like any other skill, even this can be acquired and developed.

Establish The Facts

Decisions you make should have facts and evidence as their base. If you make a decision without looking at and considering the facts, you will end up wasting a lot of time and cash in the end because it takes effort to deal with the consequences of a bad decision.

Consider Options

When it comes to rational decision making, establishing facts is the first step. The information you get will help you develop different options or courses of action. As a critical thinker, you should never put yourself in a position where you have only one option. You need to develop as many options as you can.

Evaluate the Options and Implement

Once you have chosen an option, implement the option. Decide when the option implementation will come into play, who will be responsible for doing what, and the period for implementing the option. You should also pen down evaluation criteria so that you can check whether the option you have chosen is working out well. This way, if anything is amiss, you can quickly make corrections.

Chapter Ten: How to Make a Tough Decision

So, now you know why you often fail at decision making, and the mental errors that make it such a challenging process for you. What comes next? Well, learning how to make those tough decisions that plague you at night, keeping you awake for long hours. But before we get into tips on decision-making, why is it do we often face a hard time making them, mental errors aside? You pause at a restaurant menu for half an hour, confused on what you should order. "Should I order them all?", you wonder. This hesitance, unfortunately, persists when it comes to bigger decisions at work and in our personal lives, which can be quite problematic. There are some very simple reasons why you feel this type of hesitance before making a decision.

One of the main reasons why decisions can feel so complex and tough at times is because we have this innate fear of missing out on the other choice. When you're at a restaurant, you're not sure what to get because you're worried that the choice you neglected might be better than what you're getting. If you're hiring new employees, choosing between two qualified candidates feels tough because you dread making the wrong choice.

Another reason we freeze when it is time to make a decision is dreading the consequences. It can be quite the debilitating feeling to feel the weight of responsibility resting on your shoulders, and as a result, people often get hung up on the outcomes and fail to act.

The Secrets to Making Tough Decisions with Ease

Getting the Facts Right

We have talked earlier about the importance of being well-informed, and it really shows when it comes to decision making. Critical thinking doesn't just focus on the importance of getting your facts right, but on the probability that when you have all the relevant information and facts, you will be able to make a tough decision properly because you are informed.

How can you fire an employee just based on your middle management's recommendation? You need to see their progress reports, inspect samples of their work yourself, and even have a sit-down with them to see if they are as bad as their direct managers say they are. How can you decide to buy a car out of your three possible options without meticulously reviewing each's specs and performance? It is this kind of thoroughness and attention to detail that will help you make informed decisions that lead to good results.

What Do You Believe In?

This is an important question you will need to ask yourself before making any tough decisions. Any choices stem from your own belief system and set of values, and it can be easy to lose sight of your own ideologies while struggling with a tough decision. So, always remind yourself and review your motives and values, because the answer to your dilemma often lies in reviewing your own beliefs.

Focus on a Single Feature

Also known as the "single-feature model", this is one of the best approaches that you could follow to make tough decisions. One of the biggest reasons why some decisions can be so hard is because of the fact that there are often too many options. The purpose of this model is to boil down the comparison between the various models into one single feature which you will use to make a final decision, which makes it exponentially easier.

If you have two perfect candidates for a junior vacancy in your company, focus on a single feature and make it the deciding factor. It might be years of experience, for example. So, if candidate A has 2 years of experience and B has 3, then you will go with the latter based on this model.

You should know, though, that the single-feature model might not be ideal for more complex decisions, because you ignore several other variables in the equation and focus on just one, which won't always be wise. So, use this strategy for tough decisions that don't have major consequences, and when you're pressed for time. In other words, if that last example was about a director's position, then taking just experience into consideration wouldn't be wise.

Consider the Long Run

We might be envious of people who are quite capable of thinking on their feet, making quick decisions whenever needed. But that is not necessarily a good quality to seek. When it comes to decision making, it is important that you think long term, because the consequences of complex and tough decisions are often seen and felt in the long run.

Yes, it will feel terrifying once you start looking that far ahead and figuring out the consequences of your choice, but how else will you make a tough decision if you don't think of its outcome years down the line? As we've constantly mentioned in this book, one of the most important pillars of critical thinking is being able to analyze a situation from all angles, including a future one. We tend to make decisions quickly, and we are wired to respond as fast as we could. Sometimes that works; other times, it won't. Humans are reactive creatures by nature. We respond to our circumstances and have an urge to come up with a solution before thinking it through. If you want to really make tough decisions, you will have to learn to control that side of you.

Leverage critical thinking techniques and carefully consider the repercussions of the decision you're about to make. Keep your thoughts and emotions under control. This will help you think long term and take all angles into consideration, which will exponentially improve your decision-making skills.

Create a Routine

A very efficient strategy for improving your skills is trying to reduce decision-making fatigue. Trying to come up with the right decision all the time can be very draining, and it could lead to you making poor ones just because you want to get it over with. So, what do you do to avoid this problem? Well, you create a routine for those tough but regular decisions.

It can be something as simple as not being sure which route to take to work every day. Eliminate the decision-making; choose one fixed route that you will take every day no matter what. This makes your life a bit easier, and you will be able to channel that energy into more significant and complicated decisions. Can't decide what to have for lunch at work every day? Make a routine out of eating a fruit salad for lunch every day at work. These routines will help you expend less energy on making tough but rather unimportant decisions.

What if it is an unexpected situation or choice that you encounter? Can you make a routine out of such decisions? You actually can, in a way. Deciding on what to eat for lunch every day is easy, but what would you do if you find one of your employees slacking around at work all the time? Should you talk to them about it? Should you issue a warning letter? Should you fire them on the spot? This is the type of decision that you need to routinize so you could deal with such cases with relative ease and make the right choice every time.

Here, you can follow an "if" rule to streamline your decision making. Make an "if rule" for yourself, such as "If I come out of my office 3 days in a row at 2 p.m. to find an employee sleeping on his desk or talking to his co-worker, I will talk to them. If the same thing happens two days after that, I will issue a warning letter. If this persists for the entirety of the following week, I will terminate them". That way, you create a routine out of dealing with employees who don't take the job seriously. You will obviously critically think about the situation and come up with a proper response to each scenario, but once that is done, you will be ready to make quick, informed decisions without having to waste any time or energy. Routine is often frowned upon in life, but when it comes to decision making, it can really help you get some efficient results and maintain your sanity.

Get Other Opinions

This one won't be easy for many people, but it is quite relevant, nonetheless. Who said decision making has to be an individual struggle? Sure, when it comes to those tough decisions, you will eventually be the one who decides. But critically thinking about a problem or a tough choice means understanding that you might not have the right answer, and maybe someone else does. So, why not get opinions? Talk to others and get different insights. See what they have to say and which choices they prefer and why.

Maybe someone else's insights would broaden your horizons and bring something to your attention that you have been missing. It never hurts to get a second opinion, no matter how sure of yours you are, because there isn't just one right answer. And talking to people and getting their opinions might help you take that tough decision that has been troubling you.

A final tip to this decision-making dilemma is to set a timer. It happens quite often that you will face a lot of different choices, and each could be very lucrative or very costly. You go through them all and inspect all the possible angles, and they still remain attractive. This is why it is important to set a time limitation, because you cannot linger on such decisions for long, especially in the business world. There isn't necessarily one right answer, and you will never know it until you shed your fears and move forward.

Chapter Eleven: Critical Thinking in Everyday Life

We all have great potential within us, but we don't make use of it. Most of it is lying dormant within us, or it is underdeveloped. Any improvement in thinking cannot take place if there is no conscious commitment towards learning. You cannot improve your game in basketball if you don't put in some effort to do so and the same stands true for critical thinking as well. Like any other skill, the effort is essential for its development. As long as you take your thinking for granted, there is no way in which you can unlock your true potential. Development in your thinking process is gradual, and there are several plateaus of learning that you will have to overcome and hard work is a precondition for all of this. You cannot become an excellent thinker by just wanting to become one. You will have to make a conscious decision of changing certain habits, and this will take some time. So, be patient and don't expect any change to occur overnight.

If you are interested in developing the skill of critical thinking, then you need to understand the different changes that one needs to go through in this process.

Stage 1: You are still unaware of the significant problems or pitfalls in your thinking. You aren't a reflective thinker. Most of us are stuck in this stage.

Stage2: You start developing awareness of the problems in your thinking.

Stage 3: You try working on yourself but not regularly.

Stage 4: You realize the need for regular practice.

Stage 5: You start noticing a change in the way you think.

Stage 6: You develop the ability to become insightful in your thinking.

You can progress through these stages by accepting the fact that there are specific problems in the way you think and you start putting in conscious effort to improve yourself.

Simple strategies that you can follow for developing yourself as a thinker.

Making Use of "Wasted" Time

All human beings tend to waste time; That is, we fail to make productive use of all the time we have at our disposal. Sometimes we flit from one form of diversion to another, without actually enjoying any of them. At times we get irritated about matters that are clearly beyond our control. At times, we don't plan well, and this causes a butterfly effect of negative consequences that could all have been easily avoided by simple planning. How many times have you been stuck in the rush hour traffic when you could have easily avoided this by leaving an hour earlier? Apart from all the time that we waste doing nothing, we start worrying about unnecessary things. Sometimes we regret the way we functioned in the past, or we just end up daydreaming about "what could have been" and "what can be," instead of putting in some effort to achieve results. Well, you need to realize that there is no way in which you can get all the lost time again. Instead, try focusing on all the time that you have at your disposal now. One way in which you can develop the habit of critical thinking is to make use of the time that would have normally been "wasted." Instead of spending an hour in front of the TV flipping through channels and getting bored, you can make use of this time or at least a part of it for reflecting on the day you had, the tasks you accomplished, and all that you need to achieve. Spend this time to contemplate your productivity. Here are a couple of questions that you can ask yourself:

When did I do my worst and best thinking today? What was it that I was thinking about all day long? Did I manage to come to a logical conclusion or was it all in vain? Did I indulge in any negative thinking? Did the negative thoughts just create a lot of unnecessary frustration? If I could repeat this day all over again, what would I change? Did I do something that will help me in achieving my goals? Did I accomplish anything that's worth remembering?

Spend some time answering these questions and record your observations. Over a period of time, you will notice that you have a specific pattern of thinking.

Reshaping Your Character

Select an intellectual trait like perseverance, empathy, independence, courage, humility and so on. Once you have selected a feature, try to focus on it for an entire month and cultivate it in yourself. If the trait you have opted for is humility, then start noticing whenever you admit that you are wrong. Notice if you refuse to admit this, even if the evidence points out that you are wrong. Notice when you start becoming defensive when someone tries to point out your mistake or make any corrections to your work. Observe when your arrogance is preventing you from learning something new. Whenever you notice yourself indulging in any form of negative behavior or thinking, squash such thoughts. Start reshaping your character and start incorporating desirable behavioral traits while giving up on the negative ones. You are your worst enemy, and you can prevent your growth unknowingly. So, learn to let go of all things negative.

Dealing With Your Egocentrism

Human beings are inherently egocentric. While thinking about something, we tend to favor ourselves before anyone else subconsciously. Yes, we are biased towards ourselves. In fact, you can notice your egocentric behavior on a daily basis by thinking about the following questions:

What are the circumstances under which you would favor yourself? Do I become irritable or cranky over small things? Did I do or say something that is "irrational" for merely getting my way? Did I try to impose my opinion on others? Did I ever fail to speak my mind about something I feel strongly about and then regret not doing it later on? Once you have identified the egocentric traits, you can start actively working on rationalizing yourself. Whenever you feel like you are egocentric, think what a rational person would say or do in a similar situation and the way in which that compares to what you are doing.

Redefining the Way in Which You See Things

The world that we live in is social as well as private, and every situation is "defined." The manner in which a situation is defined not only determines how you feel, but the way you act, and its implications. However, every situation can be described in multiple ways. This means that you have the power to make yourself happy and your life more fulfilling. This means that all those situations to which you attach a negative meaning can be transformed into something favorable if you want to. This strategy is about finding something positive in everything that you would have considered to be negative. Try to see the silver lining in every aspect of your life. It is all about perspectives and perceptions. If you think that something is positive, then you will feel good about it, and if you think it's negative, then you will naturally harbor negative feelings towards it.

Get in Touch with Your Emotions

Whenever you start feeling some negative emotion, ask yourself the following:

What line of thinking has led to this emotion? For instance, if you are angry, then ask yourself, what were you thinking about that has caused the anger you are feeling? What are the other ways in which I can view this situation? Every situation seems different depending on your perspective. A negative aspect makes everything seem dull and bleak, and on the other hand, a positive outlook does brighten things up. Whenever you feel a negative emotion creeping up, try to see some humor in it or rationalize it. Concentrate on the thought process that produced the negative emotion, and you can find a solution to your problem.

Analyzing the Influence of a Group on Your Life

Carefully observe the way your behavior is influenced by the group you are in. For instance, any group would have specific unwritten rules of conduct that all the members follow. There will be some form of conformity that will be enforced. Check for yourself how much this influences you and the manner in which it impacts you. Check if you are bowing too much to the pressure that is being exerted and if you are doing something just because others expect it of you.

You don't have to start practicing all the steps at once. Start out slowly and try following as many as you can. Initially, you will need to put in the conscious effort for critical thinking and, over a period, these skills will come naturally to you.

Critical Thinking and Leadership

One might assume that our leaders in government, in business, and in the nonprofit sector are strong critical thinkers. Sadly, this assumption is largely incorrect. While many leaders have at least some of the qualities of critical thinkers, few possess all of them. However, if one aspires to attain a leadership position at some point, or if one is already a leader within a field and desire to improve leadership skills, one could benefit significantly from studying and applying critical thinking skills in his life.

One of the most important characteristics of a successful leader is the he is constantly striving to learn more about himself and to seek self-improvement. Leaders work hard to look within, or, in other words, to do the introspective work as one of the most important tasks of a critical thinker. Leaders must know their strengths and their weaknesses so that they can capitalize on what they do well and work to correct areas in which they fall short. Leaders, like critical thinkers, understand that introspection and reflection are life-long processes that must be done routinely and honestly in order to keep oneself sharp.

The second skill a leader must have is that he must be proficient using the tools and the skill sets that he has. In other words, a strong leader must know how to get things done on a daily basis, using the skills he has acquired throughout his life and his training, as well as the tools available to him, technical and otherwise. Leaders, like critical thinkers, must know what they need in order to get the job done. And, just as important, they must know where to look to get what they need in order to accomplish that specific mission. Like critical thinkers, leaders are not afraid to consider various perspectives in order to solve the often-complex problems that they must address. They will seek out others' opinions, and then take the necessary time to examine the quality of each perspective, taking the time to separate the facts from the opinions. Then, and only then, are leaders able to put themselves in a much stronger position to begin to tactfully prepare a strategy to solve the problem.

The third principle of a strong leader requires leaders to develop a sense of responsibility among subordinates. Leaders engaged in the process of critical thought understand that team-building is a very important function of leadership and the best way to accomplish that goal is by working to instill a sense of comradery among those being led. This is accomplished by understanding the mission of the team as well as taking the time to learn the individual strengths of each team member and what they can contribute to the team. Then, the leader must facilitate communications among team members that focuses on information-sharing and breaking down the barriers to honest communication.

A fourth principle is that leaders must be able to make sound decisions in a timely manner. This is without a doubt one of the most important tasks in leadership. As we have learned while studying the decision-making process in our examination of critical thought processes, making a decision begins with a clear and precise statement of the problem. Then, leaders must figure out how and where to gather the information that is necessary in order to begin to think about possible solutions to the problem. Once the information has been collected, leaders must separate the facts from the perspectives and carefully consider each piece of data based upon its own merits. Once the evidence has been evaluated, then the leader must construct possible solutions and consider the likely consequences, or implications, of each possibility. Then, the leader is able to move forward with a decision and take action. This is the same process taken by practicing critical thinkers as they approach problems.

Timely decisions are important because leaders are often called upon to make difficult decisions within a very short amount of time. Even when time is short, it is important for leaders, and for critical thinkers, to make every effort to keep their mission in perspective and work as quickly as possible while working to minimize the possibility of compromising the fundamentals of sound decision-making.

A fifth principle of leadership requires leaders to always focus on setting a positive example. Leaders and critical thinkers best set examples by role-modeling examples of integrity and discipline. Leaders who practice the principles of critical thought are in an optimal position to positively affect those whom they lead because through example, they have the opportunity to motivate people to be both strong critical thinkers AND strong leaders! Leaders set examples by behaving in ways that they wish their subordinates to behave, and they are wise to remember that their position as leaders carries with it an awesome responsibility to teach, as well as to lead.

A sixth principle of leadership requires leaders to know the people they are leading and to look out for their welfare, which aligns with the concept of empathy. Leaders are at least in part responsible for those they lead. That role of responsibility may certainly be enhanced in a military environment, for example, but all leaders are at least in part responsible for educating, training, or assisting their subordinates get from Point A to Point B in some fashion. A strong leader seeks to understand those he leads from their perspective as much as that is possible and he works to accomplish that by holding individual or group meetings with them and by actively listening to what they are saying. Contrary to popular belief, a leader is not the only person doing the talking. Instead, good leaders understand that in order to understand the perspectives of their subordinates, they have to ask open-ended questions and then pay close attention to the responses.

A seventh principle of leadership reminds leaders to keep their people informed. Effective communication is absolutely critical in leadership roles and leaders must make sure that the messages they impart to their crews are clear and precise with minimal or no use of vague or ambiguous terms or phrases. Communications should be delivered in a timely manner. When preparing communications, it is important for the leader to consider his biases that may influence what he says or how he says it. He also needs to consider possible biases held by his team members and how those biases may influence their interpretations of the message he is presenting.

An eighth principle of leadership advises leaders to seek responsibility and to take responsibility for one's actions. In terms of critical thinking, this principle addresses the goal of self-direction and self-accountability. Leaders and critical thinkers are charged with offering their talents and their skill sets when they believe it is appropriate to do so, and they don't wait to be spoon-fed information when they need to solve a problem. They find out where to look and then they gather and analyze the data in a timely fashion. They also take responsibility for their shortcomings as well as their successes.

A ninth principle of leadership requires those who lead to make sure that their assigned tasks are understood and that members of their teams get the supervision they need in order to accomplish tasks successfully. This principle addresses the need for clear and precise communication and the need to understand the perspectives of the people charged with getting the job done.

Chapter Twelve: Powerful strategies to improve criticism

Keep a journal

Keeping an intellectual journal can also help you meet your goal of improving our critical thinking skills. You can write an entry every day to keep your entries regular. Each day, write an entry that describes a situation that was or is important to you. Keep track of the different problems you have managed to solve as a result of critical thinking. It must have a format that you can follow to address each problem.

Solve a problem every day

Another strategy that can help you improve your critical thinking skills is to try to solve at least one problem a day. In other words, when you start each day, you can choose a problem that you will work on in your spare time. Then take time to analyze the problem from a logical point of view, taking note of all its elements.

Redefine your point of view

Being open to considering alternative views of a situation can help you develop more refined and informed opinions. It can be difficult to accept the fact that the way you see things today may need adjustment, but it can help in the long run.

Questioning the views of others

This strategy is not about being argumentative and openly challenging people, especially in situations where this would be inappropriate. Rather, when you hear someone speak, don't always accept that the information you share, in fact.

Take time out

You must invest quality time to hone your critical thinking time. This does not mean that you spend hours each day thinking. It means that when you have a moment, for example, when you're stuck in traffic or walking from one place to another, take that time to be more productive with your thinking. By doing this, you will begin to observe certain factors about your thought process and how to reach conclusions.

Treat one problem at a time.

Critical thinking requires that your mind be clear, so don't mess it up, trying to solve too many problems at the same time. Instead, it goes through one problem at a time. Doing this will allow you to clearly establish the problem in your mind and understand what kind of problem it is.

Change your perspective

Chances are you have a way of being and seeing that is based on your personal and social interactions. From his experiences, he defines the way he understands things. For normal thinking, this is fine, but for a critical thinker, this can be very limiting. You will see that viewing the world from a perspective means that your solutions to problems tend to follow a pattern as well. This can often lead to frustration and negative emotions. Critical thinking must be able to redefine how they see the world so that they have a more open mind. This will allow finding solutions in unlikely places or scenarios.

Always question assumptions

It is easy to reach the wrong conclusions simply by forgetting to question the assumptions you have already made. Some of the best innovators in the past were people wondering if some of our fundamental human assumptions could be wrong.

Recognize the influence of groups

Groups have an unwritten and sometimes written code of conduct. Groups expect members to do and not do various things. In fact, some groups take their beliefs very seriously, and any member who goes against those beliefs is expelled from the group.

Group thinking is a major obstacle to critical thinking. You must protect yourself against that. You can protect yourself against this by acknowledging the influence of groups. Analyze the group you are in and determine what actions or behavior you expect the group and its members to comply with because each group requires some measure or level of compliance.

Take a breath and think.

Start taking it even a moment before answering a question, deciding on a course of action, or making a decision. Train yourself to think carefully, even briefly, about what you are doing and why you are doing it. The world and the people around us seem to move faster each day, but incorporating critical thoughts into their daily lives can be revealing and productive.

Talk to yourself

If you find yourself nodding or shaking your head at something said during a conversation or on the news, take a step back and consider why you made that gesture. What do you agree or disagree with? Have you always felt like this? When was the last time you thought of what you agree or disagree with as a matter of consideration, rather than something you simply agree or disagree with?

Practice asking critical questions

When do you think you would receive the best answer to a question? Would it be when you ask a general question or when you ask a specific question? And when would you expect to receive a serious and useful response? Would it be when you ask a question seriously, or when you ask it casually? If you want to receive the most useful answer to a question, the way of asking is very important. It is important that you tailor your questions in a way that causes the person you are addressing to give you relevant answers that are also helpful. Also, when trying to design questions that will help you during your research time, it is important that you frame those questions in a way that leads them to sources relevant to the topic at hand. You can also locate relevant material faster.

Obtain verifiable evidence

It is recommended that you get into the habit of learning and supporting your ideas through verifiable evidence, and also through logical thinking.

Ask questions

You can get lost when you try to think critically. You can ask so many questions that you don't even know what questions you originally asked. It is like the black hole of critical thinking. This can be exhausting and daunting. But don't stop! Go back to the basic questions and write them all down. If you write it down, the paper will remember it for you.

Know your mental processes

Self-awareness, self-awareness, self-awareness!
Knowing your own thought process is important,
especially because it moves so fast. Be aware of those
cognitive biases!

Form your own opinions

Even if you are wrong, they can give you a good starting
point. This is something like the thesis statement of your
work. It helps you decide what you're trying to prove,
but it may be totally different by the time you finish your
job due to the evidence you found.

Make a proper analysis.

It's also a great idea to get used to analyzing any
problems you have before trying to make a deduction.
Something else you must do in the same direction is
proper reasoning and also proper evaluation of situations
and challenges.

Make a reasonable interpretation.

It is important that you learn to interpret problems in-depth and in-depth as it avoids the need to accept information only at face value.

Confirm veracity of the information
You should always verify the veracity of any information you intend to use, even when you have obtained that information from published books or the Internet. Even if you are selecting information from things that you or others have observed, just check its accuracy and credibility. Let us say, in fact, that you need to verify the veracity of all the information you are considering using at all times. This helps you have more accurate information at hand.

Deal with your ego
Egocentrism can hinder critical thinking. If you are full of yourself, you will close your eyes and ears to new ideas or corrections. He tends to justify his actions, blame others, become defensive, or point out the 'deficiencies' of the person trying to correct him. Sometimes we take our self-centeredness too far by

associating with people who don't challenge us and avoid people who tend to call us.

Be innovative

Explore alternatives to find better and new solutions. You can do this by becoming innovative. Don't be afraid to try it. Don't be afraid to take risks. Your mind is a powerful tool that can generate innovation. You should not settle in your comfort zone and be happy with what you already know. Also, don't settle for what the world and the people around you already know.

Have a healthy lifestyle.

Now you may be wondering why this item appeared in an article on how to improve your critical thinking. Yes, it is necessary to live a healthy lifestyle to improve the mind. A healthy mind must be housed in a healthy body. You can never unleash your full potential if your physique is not at its best.

Be creative

Creativity is a common thing among great thinkers and successful people. In the real world, creativity is not the only luxury but a necessity and a survival skill. A critical thinker is a creative person. We all use our creativity in different ways, but we must follow a common process. Once you understand the process, you can intentionally apply it in any necessary situation. Increase your creativity and efficiency and also strengthen your initiative.

Know when to move on

You may be equipped with so much optimism that you always fight for your idea. But if things don't work out so well, change your strategy. He did not change his decision to reach his destination; you just took a different route that led to it. This is a feature that very few have. It is called flexibility. People who have this knowledge when their preferences get the best of them and are able to restructure strategies and change direction. Don't obsess over infinite possibilities. If you have done a thorough job and things are not going so well, go ahead and stay on target. Having this ability is like having a good map. It is now up to you to drive your critical mind towards your goals.

To diversify

A critical thinker embraces diversity. One of the most powerful skills of a great thinker is the ability to take advantage of diversity. We are talking here about the diversity of thought or art and the process of harnessing and maximizing different ways of thinking.

A critical factor to consider is always recognizing where you are strong and where you are not. If in a certain field, you know that you are not an expert, look for others who are. And make an effort to improve this. Listen to your thoughts and listen to the new directions that your thinking can provide. Learn to diversify and be open to the perspectives of others.

Has an open mind

It is easy to distinguish a closed-minded thinker from an open-minded one. A closed-minded thinker is not open to discussion and only firmly believes in his own set of beliefs and opinions. This is a very unacceptable attitude for someone who wants to develop a critical thinking mind. Improving your thinking involves processing new contributions. A closed-minded thinker cannot be convinced or reasoned. Imagine a glass full of water. It can no longer contain new water because it is already full.

Resist impulsiveness

Impulsive decision making is what we aim to correct by developing our thinking skills. Impulsive decision making often leads to poor and regrettable decisions. When under pressure, the temptation arises to make an impulsive decision. Some may reason that it is better to have a wrong decision than to have no decision at all. Well, that is rarely true. Indecision is an indication of thinking problems and poor decision-making skills, while impulsiveness only accelerates and ensures the consequences of poor decisions.

Eliminate ambiguity

An excellent critical thinker always exercises the power of thought to establish clarity. Ambiguity is a symptom of irrational, incomplete, and careless thinking. Now, once you experience this state, examine its principles, its insights, its promises, and the effectiveness of its thought process. Knowledge is the only weapon you can use to regain clarity from confusion and uncertainty.

Be consistent

Improving your critical thinking is a routine for constantly looking for problems in your thinking. Being consistent is a good sign of careful and deep thought. A critical thinker always applies coherence and logic in what needs to be considered. Inconsistency is only used to obscure the truth. So if you really want to improve, be consistent.

Practice empathy

A critical thinker always holds judgment until he is sure he has the right information. This is called empathy. You should not judge others until you fully understand the situation. By practicing empathy, you minimize the risk of making impulsive decisions and half-hearted conclusions. On the other hand, once you have the right information, and have thoroughly examined it, feel free to make decisions.

Know your learning style

To learn how to be more effective and supportive, learn about their learning style. This is the learning technique in which you absorb knowledge faster. For example, if you prefer practical experience, then participate in it. If you prefer lectures, readings, and debates, participate in these. If you prefer group experiences, go out and find a group.

Delete negative conversations

Negative thinking is self-talk and sub-vocal conversation that reinforces critical judgments and attitudes about you. It transmits negative images over and over again. Here are examples of this kind of thinking: I can't do anything right, I shouldn't trust anyone, I'm not as smart as everyone else, I'm ugly, I'm not loved, and school is a waste of time. When taken for granted, this type of thinking will influence your decision making in an undesirable way.

This is a serious thinking problem and therefore, should be replaced by more positive internal dialogue and self-esteem.

Have a passion for learning

Anything you want to accomplish can easily be accomplished with a burning desire, commitment, and dedication. Passion is the fuel to keep us doing what we must do. With enough passion, you will love your work with all your heart, since your mind and heart are ready to achieve your goal. Learning is the key to improving critical thinking.

Improve listening skills

Listening is a very vital skill that we often take for granted. When you start conversations, what you hear is what you get. You have probably been in a situation where, in the middle of a conversation, you realize that a person asked you a question that you did not even hear. Or maybe you daydream during a discussion in the classroom. It happens to all of us; It indicates our deficiency in this ability. The better you listen; The more information you will get. With more information comes better decisions.

Always keep perspective

Maintaining a sense of perspective in the midst of an important issue is characteristic of a critical thinker. Do not balance in any situation and always see the matter on a larger scale. Ask yourself this question; Is it really as critical as it is right now?

Check your emotions

Emotions affect how you think. Many of us make spontaneous decisions of the moment based on our emotions of that moment, and then we end up regretting those decisions when we rationally think about it later. Some of us go one step further and allow negative thinking to depress us and prevent us from making decisions that will change our situation. This should not be the case. You need to check your emotions.

Developing intellectual humility

As a critical thinker, you must take pride in developing critical thinking skills and strive to become a better thinker. However, this should not lead you to think that you are immune to mistakes. If you develop intellectual arrogance, you will be setting yourself up for failure because eventually, your arrogance will cloud your judgment, and you will begin to think that your opinion is the only correct one.

Be aware of your thought processes.

The phenomenon of human thought is quite impressive. However, automation and speed can actually stop us when we try to think more critically. Our minds tend to search for shortcuts to discover what is happening in our world or the immediate situation. When we had to fight animals or hunt to survive, this was beneficial, but now it can be an obstacle in everyday decision-making situations. An effective critical thinker already knows their own cognitive biases along with any possible biases that may be influencing their solutions and decisions. We all have prejudices, and becoming aware of them is what contributes to critical thinking.

Always make sure you think of yourself.
People often make the mistake of getting so caught up in reading and research that they forget to form their own ideas. This does not mean being arrogant or overconfident, but simply recognizing that to answer difficult questions, you must think on your own.

Remember that nobody is perfect.
It is impossible for a human being to think critically literally all the time, so remember this and be easy on yourself, especially at first. We all have irrational

thoughts sometimes. Critical thinking is a tool, not the default way to experience life.

Chapter Thirteen: Tips on how to improve your child's critical thinking skills

You will note that most of the children in honor, AP or other advanced placement classes are usually children who have developed their critical thinking skills. These children can usually look at things in more than one way and dissect information more critically. Most of these children receive high-quality examinations and perform very well. Although they were born with many of their intellectual abilities, many of their abilities were also taught and mastered. Any child can, therefore, develop his or her critical thinking and enhance his or her understanding of the information that he or she receives at and outside school.

Activities to support your child – Do not only encourage children to waste their entire time watching TV or playing video games over the long summer break and delegate them to work. Enable your children to work to develop their critical thinking skills. There are just a few examples below.

1. Read and analyze a book Together-Have your children read a book suitable for age and levels of reading and

then write a book review stating what they liked and why. The "why" is the most important thing, because it encourages your kids to think more objectively about why they developed those opinions. You should also have read the novel. Ensure that the author discusses various components-i.e. the information presented and the different methods used by the author, such as symbols, metaphors, foreshadows, moods, etc.

2. Assign your kids an argumentative research paper, then change it-make your kids choose a semi-controversial subject (you may want to choose the subject for them), then write to your kids as logically as possible why they are for it, and then write another paper explaining why they are against it. When your children have finished writing both papers, let them show what they have discovered during their writing. Then work together to improve their two papers – make constructive criticism, while also recognizing the positive.

a. Make sure your children remember that there are different ways to look at things and that they should learn to take critical information and not to allow emotions to dictate their opinions.

b. Objectivity is important to being a rational thinker; emotions also impede our analytical thought.

c. The best arguments are those in which the writer can predict what the opposing side will argue about and thus can take these arguments forward.

3. Analyze an artwork-have your kids analyze an important artwork. Ask your children questions about this piece so that they can think critically and see art in a different way. What is the viewpoint? Was the painting effective for the desired view? Why not? Why or why not? Read the subtitle that goes with the piece of art or any other relevant information in order for the artist and his work to be better understood. Bear in mind that art is very subjective. The main idea is to get your child to try critically and newly to interpret an image.

4. Analyze the source - Write your children's research paper. When you read, your children evaluate what the writer's point is-does the writer seeks to persuade you? Take note of the sources given by the author, considering whether and why they are accurate. Also, note the inconsistencies or contradictions contained in the post. Is the article based mainly on opinion, or does

the writer give him sufficient factual and objective information to demonstrate his argument? Helps your children analyze the information presented critically and objectively; let them know your thinking process as you analyze the paper.

Common Misconceptions and Mistakes in Critical Thinking

Critical thinking entails taking content apart to analyze it separately then putting it back with evidence while correlating it to the initial subject matter. Many people use the term critical thinking loosely. Therefore, several misconceptions and mistakes exist, that people believe in or carry out in the name of critical thinking.

For starters, several people think that critical thinking is applicable only in school. Others do not know how to do it as well as when and where they can apply critical thinking. Below, we try to identify some of the misconceptions surrounding critical thinking and the common mistakes people make that affect critical thinking.

Common misconceptions of critical thinking

It is essential to understand these misconceptions, avoid them, and even point them out whenever an individual appears to have fallen prey to some of them. The most common include:

Critical thinking is only used in academics and certain courses

People usually learn and use critical thinking in classroom set-ups, but the truth is it can happen anywhere, including in other subjects other than English and philosophy subjects. It is an important skill, and more and more employers slowly realize the importance of hiring people with critical thinking skills. That said, school curriculums should encourage students to develop this skill, as it is practical in history, science, law, engineering, journalism, athletics, and very many other areas.

Critical thinking is not for children

People should never underestimate children, whether they are in preschool or high school. They are as much capable of critical thinking as adults are. Some would say that they are even better at it than adults are because their minds are free from the preconceptions most grownups have developed over the years, which means that they can create their perspective of things. Therefore, instead of enforcing certain believes and ideas, children should be encouraged to think critically and form their judgment.

People from low-income backgrounds cannot think critically

Although children from low-income family set-ups do not have access to classrooms or proper education, they are still very capable of critical thinking. Some, with the help of their guardians, can develop this skill at home and eventually become very successful in life. Involving these children in extracurricular activities and clubs to foster their skills can prove to be beneficial in closing the gap between the rich and poor.

Critical thinking is hard work

Critical thinking does not necessarily have to be complicated. People should look at it as an opportunity to display knowledge and creativity rather than work. Those who find it difficult should keep in mind that the whole point of critical thinking is to dissect that which is hard. An individual may take time to process and synthesize the information, but once he or she understands each bit, the bigger picture can fall into place. Collective critical thinking is even easier and more informative. It is beneficial to the group that lacks the knowledge and as well as the knowledgeable lot.

Answering multiple-choice questions is somehow critical thinking

Answering a multiple-choice question or engaging in step-by-step tasks does not necessarily involve critical thinking. Listening to a person formulating his or her answers rather than directing him or her to a particular answer is much more insightful to the student and teacher. There might be some critical thinking involved in arriving at the best answer, but giving a person more leeway to think about the question and all the possible solutions encourages extensive thinking and, thus, deeper understanding. Systematically tasks also limit people in terms of reasoning and gathering knowledge, which is not what critical thinking is about. Allowing for extensive research and conclusion of what is relevant and what is not leads to deeper learning.

Critical thinking is the same as excellent thinking

Thinking excellent can be an essential part of thinking, but people should not confuse it with critical thinking. Critical thinking is not always present whenever people experience or achieve good results.

It is possible to produce excellent ideas and strategies without understanding the process. Students can solve complex problems and be actively engaged in their course, but this does not mean that they fully understand what their course entails, why it is essential, and how it is applicable. This right here is why teachers should encourage explicit thinking rather than excellent thinking to broaden their student's mindset.

Knowledge is a prerequisite in critical thinking

Knowledge in critical thinking can prove to be essential but is not necessarily a prerequisite. People can acquire knowledge through critical thinking, but they can also use the knowledge they have in analytical thinking. Having background knowledge in a particular area can prove to be helpful, but gathering information in critical thinking can also result in a deeper understanding.

Critical thinking occurs every time during high order learning

Critical thinking does not always take place every time students are required to interpret information and justify their thinking. Teachers can request students to analyze information but only for extending their foundational knowledge. However, if they get to deeper analysis and applications, then they are practicing critical thinking.

Critical thinking only involves criticism and arguments

Although critical thinking may lead to disapproval of people's ideas, people should view it as a way of analyzing information and conducting a close review of data presented rather than criticism of people's ideas. However, an individual should consider every insight before dismissing anything. In the end and thanks to critical thinking, people can understand one another's perspective and settle only on the best solution.

In addition to having numerous misconceptions concerning critical thinking, some people go further to attempt to think or reason critically in the wrong way. Some people fall into the trap of some of these common mistakes, and without an open mind and access to proper guidance, some are sure to continue making the same mistakes in the name of critical thinking. Some of the most common mistakes include:

Thinking with emotions rather than logic

People must learn to filter their emotions to be effective critical thinkers. Emotions are essential in decision-making, but they should not blind people from getting to the truth. Notably, group discussions can sometimes get heated, and in worse case scenarios, confrontational but critical thinking embraces such disagreements as long as people maintain respect for one another's opinions and do not involve personal emotions. Additionally, our perception of other people and beliefs should not prevent us from listening, collecting, or assessing information and coming to logical conclusions.

Favoring traditions

The fact that a tradition has been present for a long time does not necessarily make it true. Proper evidence is required to support a traditional belief if you want to prove whether the tradition is based on the truth or a lie. This does not mean that critical thinkers should abandon their traditional beliefs; on the contrary, it means that they should hold on to them but with good reasons and facts. The traditions that might not be true but have a positive outcome are also good opportunities for critical thinkers to consider the greater good.

Biasness

If a decision has been arrived at using bias information, then critical thinking has not taken place. Critical thinkers are objective and do not make decisions based on favoritism. Another mistake potential critical thinkers are guilty of is dismissing information given by a person that they think is bias.

Equivocation

Using certain words or phrases without understanding their true meaning can distort the purpose of information relayed to another person. Equivocation mostly occurs in conversation, debates, and arguments, and if people are not consciously aware of their word choice, then they can mislead people into making the wrong conclusions. Misinterpretation of words and phrases can also lead people to arrive at incorrect findings.

Failure to look at all perspectives

Critical thinking entails doing extensive research. This means continuing to gather information even if the first evidence collected confirms an ideology. Critical thinking does not assume that the current evidence is better than any other evidence that other people might have collected; it encourages more research. If an individual encounters conflicting evidence, no dismissal occurs; instead, people gather more information until there is sufficient data to conclude.

Dismissing people's perspectives

Critical thinkers allow themselves the opportunity to see things from other people's perspectives. They take into consideration other people's opinions and advice, research the same, and then draw sensible conclusions. They do not make the mistake of distorting other people's beliefs and statements as it prevents people from getting to the truth. Critical thinkers believe that other people's perspectives are just as critical as their own.

Ignorance

Just because a person fails to obtain evidence does not mean that it does not exist. Critical thinkers look for both supporting and undermining proof before concluding about a specific subject matter. They do not ignore any information they encounter. They review it and determine its credibility. If an individual finds a particular piece of information to be credible and useful, he or she picks it as evidence. Such an individual can dismiss any irrelevant or inaccurate information only after careful consideration.

Not diving deep enough

Critical thinking requires looking deep into the source of data rather than the face value of the data. Critical thinkers do not just gather data; they intensely scrutinize it to determine its accuracy. They are also eager to learn about the assumptions they have made in the information collected.

Ignoring the bigger picture

As critical thinkers dissect information and dive deep into research and collection of data, they always have in mind why they are doing what they are doing and how every small piece of the puzzle they come across fits into the big picture. Once critical thinkers collect all the facts and data they have received, they link it together and remember to include all the necessary evidence. They do not forget the purpose of their research at any point.

Concluding before gathering all the facts and data

Critical thinking takes a lot of effort and time. Only collecting information from a few sources and failing to exhaust research is not acceptable in critical thinking. Any person involved in critical thinking must be ready for extensive research and a thorough collection of data.

Rushing to take action

Guesswork, hearsay, and untrustworthy sources are short cuts and do not allow for the proper gathering of information required in critical thinking. Rushing to conclude such short cuts is not a proper procedure. People can arrive at a proper conclusion by collecting credible information, compiling it and eliminating all other possible options through a thorough thought selection process.

Not asking for help

Critical thinkers believe that two heads are better than one. Brainstorming with a group of people can give a person other perspectives that they had not thought of. Picking other people's brains also makes the process fun and enjoyable. It can also help in justifying or dismissing any evidence collected, thus narrowing down the viable options.

It is possible for anyone, regardless of how much he or she wants to apply critical thinking and reasoning in every situation, to find him or herself giving in to some of the above misconceptions and entertaining some of the mistakes. What is essential for anyone is to try as hard as possible to apply the skills and to do it as often as possible. With enough practice, the critical way of thinking can sure become a lifestyle.

Sound and Cogent Arguments

We all engage in arguments in our day-to-day lives. When we make a claim and support it with enough reasons as to why we are doing so, we are making an argument. For example, if you are an employee and you're persuading your employer to increase your salary using your performance record, then you have made an argument.

There are two types of logical arguments – inductive and deductive arguments. The test of an argument is evaluated by its soundness, validity, reliability, and strength.

Deductive arguments – this is an argument with true statements that will result in a true conclusion. Deductive arguments can be valid or invalid. Valid arguments with true premises are said to be sound. Example:

- All men are mortal

- Socrates is a man; therefore, Socrates is mortal

Inductive arguments – this argument looks at the data available and concludes examining the data. Inductive arguments can be strong or weak. Strong arguments with true premises are referred to as cogent. Example of an inductive argument:

This cat is black. That cat is black. The third cat is black; therefore, all cats are black.

Sound Arguments

This is a valid argument that has true premises; hence, the conclusion should be believed. A sound argument should always have a valid conclusion.

Example:

- All rabbits are mammals.

- Bunny is a rabbit.

- Therefore, Bunny is a mammal.

In this case, the premises are true, so the conclusion is true. Sound arguments are good arguments because you are sure to get the right conclusions.

Cogent Arguments

This is a strong argument, which has true premises. This is a good argument since the premises are true and have relevant information, so it is logically valid.

Example:

- If it is raining, then the ground is wet.

- It is raining.

- Therefore, the ground is wet.

Conclusion

It is with the utmost hope that you have found this book to be as informative, useful, and actionable as it was intended to be. When you made it a point to pick up this book and read, you dedicated yourself to learning how to think in a way that was critical, perhaps not knowing the benefits that would come along with it. Critical thinking is crucial to success in this day and age, both for adults and children alike, and when you make it a point to develop your own critical thinking abilities, you will find that you are much happier than you were before.

Critical thinking itself, as you have learned, comes with several benefits of its own. When you can think critically, you are able to communicate better, which facilitates better relationships with others. This leads to improved happiness and fulfillment. When you are able to think critically, you can identify solutions to problems that you did not realize were as difficult to solve as they were, and you are able to do so without giving up.

Critical thinkers utilize their abilities constantly—you can figure out how to make your decisions, how to interact with others, and why you should think or act in a certain way all because you learned how to think critically. You learned how to consider situations around you in ways that are deliberate, attentive to detail, meticulous, and meant to bring you closer to solving any problems that you have encountered, always managing to make your way to the right decision, even if you have to hit some roadblocks along the way. Nevertheless, when you become a critical thinker, one thing is for sure: You become intelligent, informed, and capable of making judgments that are trustworthy and should be valued by others.

From here, you have several options. You can continue to work on understanding your own ability to think critically. You could look into the development of emotional intelligence, another soft skill that is quite closely related to critical thinking. You could choose to take classes on the subject, read into philosophy, or other schools of thought that require critical thinking to be at the forefront of your mind. No matter what it is that you choose to do, however, you can do so with confidence.

If what comes next is that you choose to pursue critical thinking skills for your child, you may decide that what you will do is find a child-specific critical thinking book in order to begin developing a list of activities that you can do with your child to develop his or her own critical thinking capacity. If that is the path that you take, know that you are giving your child a great opportunity and a tool that will serve him or her well in life, thanks to your willingness to put in the effort and teach these skills.

No matter what, good luck on your future endeavors. No matter what you have chosen, you now have the skills that you will need to see it to fruition with the steps provided in how to think critically. Good luck once more and thank you for letting me join you in this process!

Emily Campbell